A CREATIVE STEP-BY-STEP GUIDE TO

THE WATER
GARDEN

A CREATIVE STEP-BY-STEP GUIDE TO

THE WATER
GARDEN

Author
Yvonne Rees

Photographer
Neil Sutherland

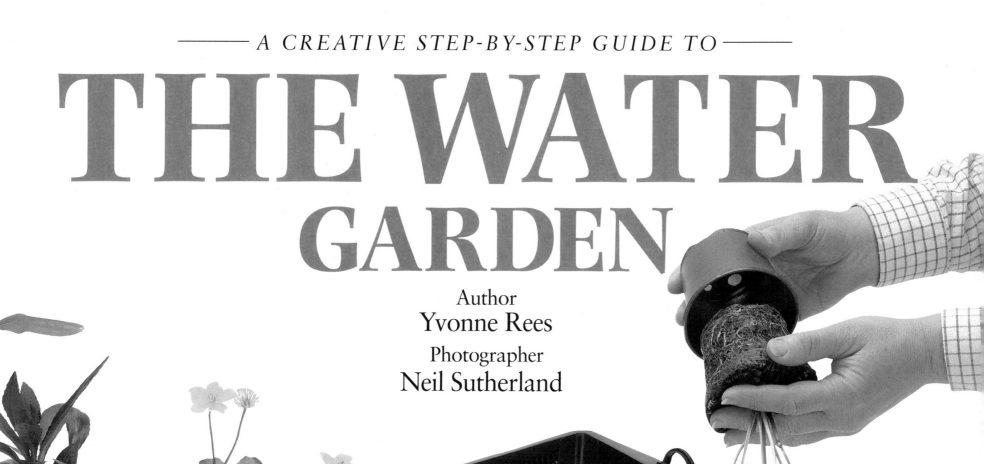

COOMBE BOOKS

Credits

Edited and designed: Ideas into Print
Photographs: Neil Sutherland
Photographic location: Stapeley Water Gardens, Cheshire
Typesetting: Ideas into Print and Ash Setting and Printing
Production Director: Gerald Hughes
Production: Ruth Arthur, Sally Connolly, Neil Randles

THE AUTHOR

Yvonne Rees has been involved with water gardening, garden design and garden maintenance for over 20 years. She designs and installs ponds and has written several books on water gardening, as well as lecturing and broadcasting on the subject.

THE PHOTOGRAPHER

Neil Sutherland has more than 25 years experience in a wide range of photographic fields, including still-life, portraiture, reportage, natural history, cookery, landscape and travel. His work has been published in countless books and magazines throughout the world.

Half-title page: The sounds and reflections of a rippling cascade add another dimension to the garden.
Title page: You can buy a wide variety of marginal plants to suit ponds and pools of all shapes and sizes.
Copyright page: A tropical water lily, such as *Nymphaea* 'Director George T. Moore', lends an exotic touch.
Contents page: A selection of primulas, ideal as bog plants.

CLB 3312

This edition published in 1998 by Coombe Books
© 1994 Colour Library Books Ltd, Godalming, Surrey
Printed and bound in Singapore by Tien Wah Press (PTE.) Ltd.
ISBN 1-85833-191-9

CONTENTS

THE PLEASURES OF WATER GARDENING

A water feature in the garden is an instant focal point; the gleam of a pond, the sparkle of a fountain or the fantastic shapes and colors of lush water plants are irresistible. Because water is so adaptable, any size, shape or style of garden can easily incorporate a stunning feature if you only have the confidence to include it in your plans, and if you take the time and trouble to plan it properly. A large plot offers the chance to enjoy a good-sized pond, complete with a wide range of plants, a bog garden, maybe a bridge or stepping stones leading to an additional platform or island area. Smaller ponds for more moderate gardens can still offer a scaled-down range of exciting plants and moving water features, such as a fountain or a waterfall. Even a tiny patio or courtyard could be transformed by a wall-mounted water spout, a small bubble fountain or a pool or bog garden in a barrel. As well as looking good, a water feature will attract a wide range of wildlife to your garden, not just frogs and toads, but also insects, such as dragonflies, different species of birds, and small mammals. A pool or coolly splashing fountain has a wonderful relaxing effect, too, converting your garden into an excellent retreat and an escape from the stress of everyday life. Best of all, once installed and providing it is correctly constructed, a water feature is one of the easiest garden features to maintain.

Left: Lilies and hostas. **Right:** Aponogeton distachyos, *the water hawthorn.*

Choosing a pool style

A water feature in the garden can be so versatile, that its size and style are limited only by your courage and imagination. If you do not find a preformed pool that inspires you, you can create virtually any kind of pool you please with the latest flexible liners. Of course, there are some practical restrictions to consider (see page 18), but choosing the right style is crucial, for whatever its size and position, water is a natural focal point; that flash of light reflecting the brightness and movement of the sky is guaranteed to capture the attention, and the wealth of interest a pool can offer is sure to hold it. Once installed, this is where you will want to spend most of your garden time, so make sure your new water feature is in keeping with the rest of your plants and features. The smart terrace or patio, or the formally designed garden with its regular beds and borders, cries out for a suitably edged formal pool, either raised or sunken, in any manner of geometric shapes, from squares to rectangles and even circles and hexagons. Two or more formal pools can often be successfully linked, by interlocking similar shapes, or by arranging pools on different levels with the water spilling from one to another by means of a water pump. The informal pool by comparison, should be a profusion of plants, a veritable jungle of lush moisture-lovers, such as marsh marigolds, astilbe, mimulus, reeds and rushes.

Right: This well-planted narrow pool follows the edge of the patio and provides the perfect link between the paving and garden.

Below: A bold approach often pays off. This large koi pool successfully dominates a modest-sized plot, featuring a timber-decked patio linked to the rest of the garden via a substantial bridge.

Above: Interlocking raised pools on two levels make a perfectly integrated patio feature and can be linked by a small cascade to provide extra interest.

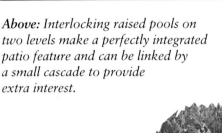

Above: Lush planting with marginals and bog plants is the making of an informal pond and produces a focal point anywhere in the garden.

Left: A wildlife pond such as this might be successfully integrated into the corner of a more formal garden and can be specifically designed to attract a wide range of birds, insects and small mammals.

Above: Even the smallest pond will soon offer a fascinating variety of wildlife for you to observe at your leisure. Frogs, toads and newts will be attracted to this new habitat.

Choosing a good site

Once installed, a pool can be relatively trouble-free, providing you position and build it correctly. Although there are few locations where a pool is completely impractical, if you want to grow a few plants and maintain a healthy ecological balance in the water, you are advised to choose an open, sunny site away from any deciduous trees that can make such a mess of the water in the fall. Consider, too, when planning a sunken pool, that there may be problems under the ground, such as old foundations, power cables or drains. If re-siting any of these is too expensive, or a sunken pool is just not practical, then you may have to consider a raised pool. Sometimes the ideal site for a pool suggests itself: within the design of a patio, for example, or where there is a natural damp depression in the ground. Often a pool can be tucked logically into the existing contours of the garden, into the angle of a corner, or used to create a parallel with the straight edges of a paved area or patio. It makes sense to choose a site as close to the house as possible. This not only gives you instant access to the poolside, but also means that you can see and enjoy the pond from the comfort of your home in bad weather; it will be closer to a power source for running pumps and lighting, too. You can also create wonderful reflections of your house lit up at night in the water surface. Another important consideration if you have a young family is that pools and ponds must be positioned where they can be safely fenced off. If you find it difficult to imagine the size and shape of the finished pool in the context of your garden, try drawing up a scaled diagram, then use pegs and string or an old hosepipe to sketch out the shape on the ground.

Right: For a pool to look good and in keeping with its surroundings, ensure that its shape and position fit the overall plan of your garden and that plants and construction materials are linked visually to nearby features.

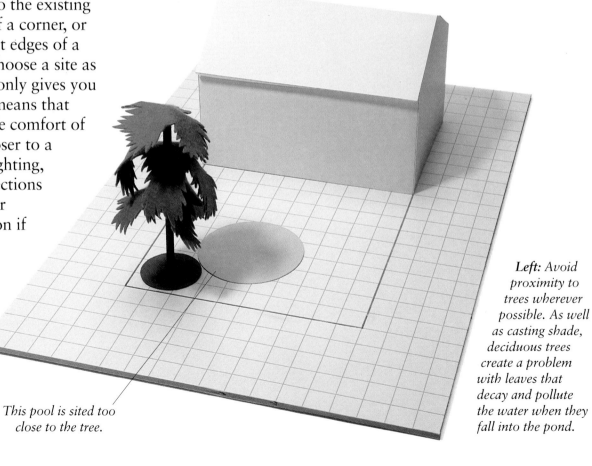

This pool is sited too close to the tree.

Left: Avoid proximity to trees wherever possible. As well as casting shade, deciduous trees create a problem with leaves that decay and pollute the water when they fall into the pond.

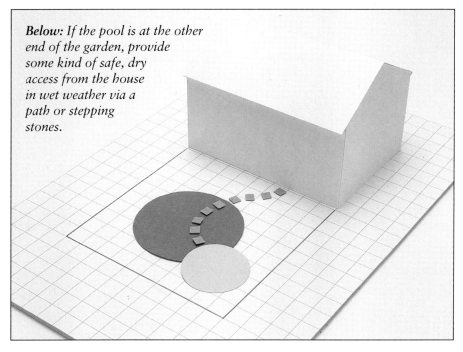

Below: *If the pool is at the other end of the garden, provide some kind of safe, dry access from the house in wet weather via a path or stepping stones.*

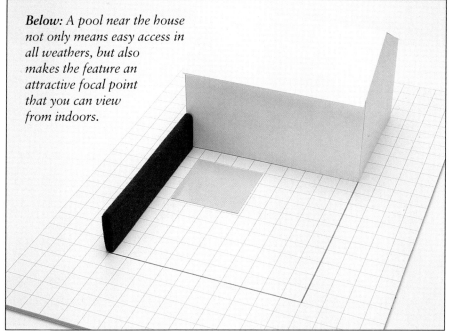

Below: *A pool near the house not only means easy access in all weathers, but also makes the feature an attractive focal point that you can view from indoors.*

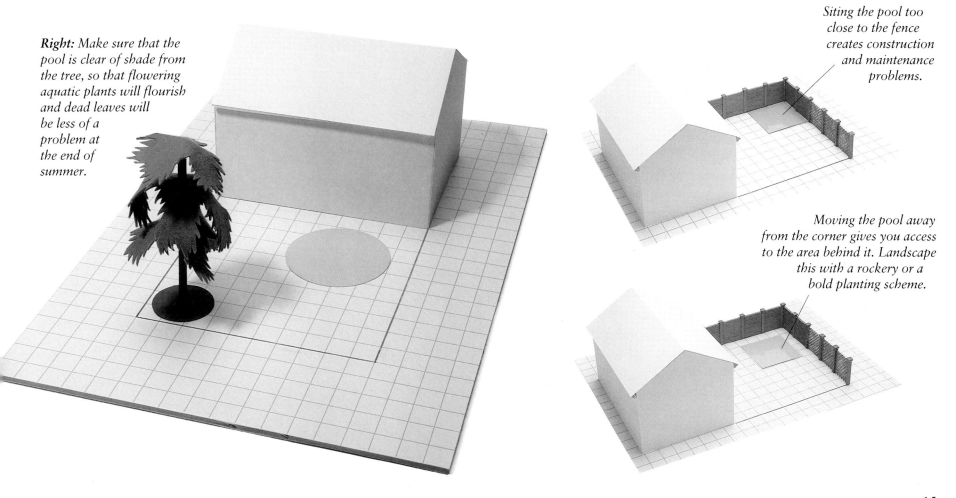

Right: *Make sure that the pool is clear of shade from the tree, so that flowering aquatic plants will flourish and dead leaves will be less of a problem at the end of summer.*

Siting the pool too close to the fence creates construction and maintenance problems.

Moving the pool away from the corner gives you access to the area behind it. Landscape this with a rockery or a bold planting scheme.

Looking after a pond

Once established, a properly constructed and well-planned pond requires very little maintenance. Most water plants grow prolifically and are not prone to pests and diseases. Just keep an eye open for lily beetle or aphids on your water lilies and hose them into the water for the fish to eat. In fact, the plants in and around your pond will grow rather too well and thinning out and cutting back is one task you will have to tackle at least annually. Take this opportunity to propagate new plants by taking cuttings or dividing roots. If you have the ecological balance right, the water should look after itself. If not, and you get a spell of prolonged sunshine, it may turn green with scum - actually overactive algae. This is more a problem with smaller pools; you can add chemicals as a short-term solution or install a water filter as described on page 34. The actual pond construction should last many years without any need for repair. It is possible to mend cracks in concrete and rips in lining material using the appropriate repair kit, but the pond will have to be emptied and drained. Never do this at the end of the summer when pond life is just settling down to weather the winter. Make winter care for your pond a routine. Remove any dead leaves with a rake or net at the end of summer, clear away any dead plant material to prevent it polluting the water and install a small pond heater if you are worried for your fish. Ponds deeper than 24in(60cm) should not freeze totally, so this will not be a problem. A moving water feature, such as a fountain or waterfall, will also keep the water relatively unfrozen. If kept running permanently, you could leave a submersible pump in the pond during the winter. Otherwise remove and clean it and store it in a dry shed.

Below: Fish prefer clean water and plenty of cover for protection and shade. The plastic strings here are to deter herons, which can be a nuisance poaching your livestock.

Right: If your pond should freeze over in winter, never bang the ice to crack it; you will stun the fish and it will freeze over again anyway. For small pools, a heater is economical to run.

Avoiding green water

Green scummy water is the scourge of small ponds. You can avoid the problem if you keep the water free from dead or decaying plant material. Cover the pool with a net to catch falling leaves at the end of the growing season. Making sure the surface is partially covered by floating plants and water lilies helps shade out the light and heat that algae thrive on. If you are still getting problems, then you may have to install a biological filter.

Above and right: Sunshine encourages algae, causing green scummy water. Twirl algal threads out on a stick.

Below: *If you get the ecological balance right, both pool and water plants will flourish with minimum maintenance. It may take more than one season to be successful.*

Right: *Pond plants, such as these* Iris laevigata 'Variegata' *and* Primula pulverulenta *quickly become overgrown. Keep rampant plants in check during the growing season.*

Cut through the rootstock with a sharp knife to divide the original clump into smaller plants.

Right: *Some marginal plants, such as iris, grow from a tuberous rootstock, which is easy to divide. Dig up the overgrown plant using two garden forks and split the roots or tubers to give established plants a new lease of life.*

Below: *As a bonus, you could create several new plants from the old root material. Each one of these should grow away healthily.*

17

Lining options

Unless you are paying a professional to design and/or excavate your pool, waterproofing it with some kind of lining material is going to be your greatest expense. There are no really cheap options: the less expensive materials will still take a fair slice of your budget, and it has to be considered that they do not perform as well as those at the top of the range. Compromising on size and style is the only way you can reasonably cut costs. Another very important point to bear in mind before you buy is that the more accurate your measurements, the less wastage there is, so do double check all your calculations. The easiest type of liners to buy are the preformed pools, which are available in a choice of sizes and shapes, including both formal and informal styles. Most incorporate a marginal shelf for plants. The cheapest of these are made of thin plastic and are fairly flimsy so do need handling and installing carefully. Their durability is fairly limited, too. Rigid pools are also available in much thicker plastic and these should last for many years. Much stronger but more expensive are the preformed GRP (glass reinforced plastic) shapes, which can be bought in an equally wide variety of styles to suit every garden.

The most popular type of liner is currently the flexible type: you buy it in a piece, or off a roll, and it stretches to fit every contour of your excavation. The inexpensive forms of PVC (polyvinyl chloride) and polyethylene (polythene) liners can be prone to fading or splitting after a few years of exposure to strong sunlight and cold winters. Several other plastic formulations are sold for pools and these are often supplied with a guarantee of up to 20 years. If you intend your feature to be permanent, you may wish to choose a butyl rubber liner, a highly durable material available in various thicknesses.

A selection of lining materials

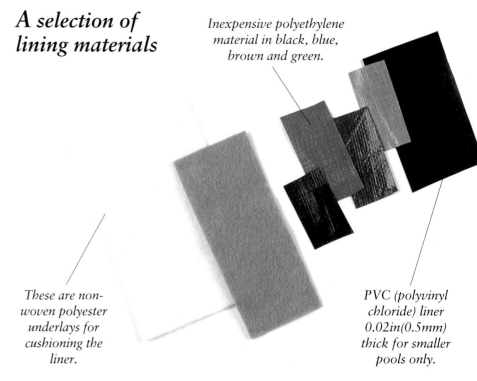

Inexpensive polyethylene material in black, blue, brown and green.

These are non-woven polyester underlays for cushioning the liner.

PVC (polyvinyl chloride) liner 0.02in(0.5mm) thick for smaller pools only.

Left: *This informal pool has been made with a rigid plastic liner. The pebble edging planted with creeping ground cover protects the pool from grass clippings.*

This rigid plastic shell is typical of a wide range of preformed shapes you can buy to enable you to create an 'instant' pond in your garden.

Once installed, you can disguise the rim with an edging of your choice.

Using concrete

Some people still favor concrete for lining a pool. It is certainly strong and can be watertight providing it is correctly mixed and applied. Concreting a pool is not a job for a novice. Even the simplest design will need to incorporate some reinforcing material. The components must be kept clean and be accurately measured, and the work carried out when there is no risk of frost or extremely dry, sunny weather.

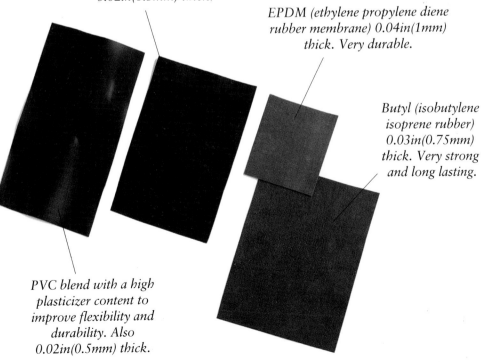

A depth of at least 24in(60cm) here will enable fish to overwinter in ice-free water.

Most rigid pool have a shelf at the right depth to support pots of marginal plants.

LDPE (low-density polyethylene) liner 0.02in(0.5mm) thick.

EPDM (ethylene propylene diene rubber membrane) 0.04in(1mm) thick. Very durable.

Butyl (isobutylene isoprene rubber) 0.03in(0.75mm) thick. Very strong and long lasting.

PVC blend with a high plasticizer content to improve flexibility and durability. Also 0.02in(0.5mm) thick.

Raised pools

The big advantage of a raised pool is that there is no digging and relatively little disturbance to the garden or patio. You can easily integrate a raised pool with other features, such as seating and raised beds. There may be practical reasons why a raised pool is preferable: a difficult site with bedrock just below the surface; a high water table; a sloping garden or simply a small budget. If you want to make a raised pool using a liner or a preformed unit, it is best to choose a circular or oval shape to help the pool withstand the pressure of water; without the support of soil around it, a square-edged design would be prone to splitting or breaking down at the corners. On a formal patio,

Above *A formal raised pool with a fountain makes an excellent focal point to the patio, drive or lawn.*

you can edge the pool with pavers or brick to match the patio, and remember that the wide rim of coping stones makes a handy place to sit and watch the water or to stand pots of suitable plants.

Preparing a liner pool

Mark out the shape of your proposed pool on the grass or soil using a hosepipe or pegs and string. This allows you to walk round the area and view it from every angle - even from above if you can see from a nearby window - and adjust the outline until you are satisfied it looks right. Cut turfs from the area using a sharp-edged spade, lift and roll them root side out, and keep them damp until you need them around the pool or elsewhere in the garden. Next remove the topsoil, taking care not to mix it with any subsoil or rubble, and also putting it to one side for further use. You can now begin the serious digging of the subsoil. If you have not planned to use it to contour the area around the pool or to create other raised features, arrange for the waste to be taken away. Dig out the subsoil to your required depth - a minimum of 24in(60cm) and usually no more than about 48in(120cm). Remember to incorporate a shelf for marginal plants about 10in(25cm) below the final water level. About 12in(30cm) wide should be sufficient for positioning plant baskets. Most importantly, you must make sure your excavations are completely level; if the sides vary in height, the pool will look very strange once it is filled with water. The easiest way to achieve this is to knock a 48in(120cm) post into the center of your pool area. Use this to balance one end of a straight edge extended from a series of small 12in(30cm) pegs or posts sited around the edge of the bank. Place a spirit level along the top to show you where any adjustments need to be made to ensure a level finish. When the excavations are complete and the sides are level, go over the base and sides by hand, making sure there are no major bumps or hollows, and remove any sharp stones that might damage your liner.

Above: The edge of the flexible liner is just visible at the back margin of this small informal pool. Being black helps it to blend in with the water surface.

1 *To protect the liner against damage use a custom-made pond cushioning material or use a layer of sand, old carpet, sacking or loft insulation material, as here.*

Use gloves when handling this - the fibers can irritate skin.

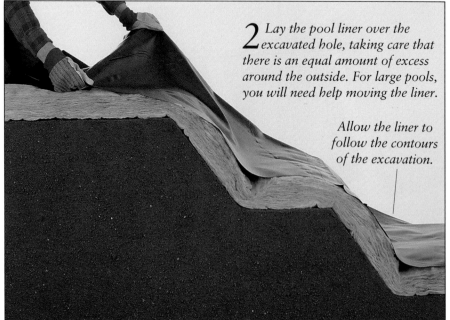

2 *Lay the pool liner over the excavated hole, taking care that there is an equal amount of excess around the outside. For large pools, you will need help moving the liner.*

Allow the liner to follow the contours of the excavation.

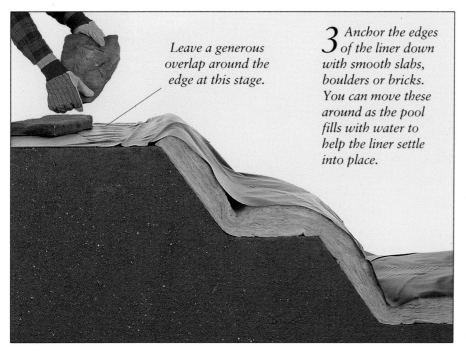

Leave a generous overlap around the edge at this stage.

3 Anchor the edges of the liner down with smooth slabs, boulders or bricks. You can move these around as the pool fills with water to help the liner settle into place.

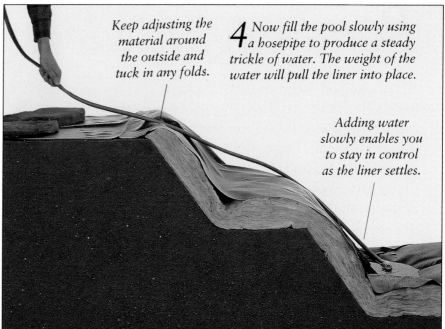

Keep adjusting the material around the outside and tuck in any folds.

4 Now fill the pool slowly using a hosepipe to produce a steady trickle of water. The weight of the water will pull the liner into place.

Adding water slowly enables you to stay in control as the liner settles.

This marginal shelf is 12in(30cm) wide with about 10in(25cm) of water above it.

5 This profile represents a small liner pool once it has been filled for the first time. This setup is used on the following pages to show edging options and how to install pumps.

6 When the pool has filled to its level, cut away any excess, leaving about 12in(30cm) to be anchored and hidden by your choice of edging.

The maximum depth of water in the middle of the pool is 24in(60cm).

How much liner?

Add twice the maximum depth of the pool to both the overall length and width. Thus, a pool 10ft x 6ft x 2ft deep (3 x 1.8 x 0.6m) needs a liner 14 x 10ft (4.2 x 3m). Liner is flexible and stretches to fit with the weight of the water, so there is no need to allow for the gentle contouring of an informal pool or the extra few inches of a marginal shelf.

Pond edging ideas

Marginal and moisture-loving plants do an excellent job of disguising and softening the edge of ponds, especially where you want to achieve a natural informal look. But you cannot plant them all the way round; you need access to the water, maybe even a place to sit near the water's edge, where you can relax and observe plants and wildlife at close quarters. Grassy banks are perfect for informal ponds and streams being complementary to both plants and other natural materials, such as stone and timber. You could even use it in a formal way where a geometrically shaped pool is set into a lawn. The grass can be inset with other elements, such as bricks or pavers for a formal look or random stone or slabs for a more natural style. A wide flat stone close by the water's edge makes a useful seat or hard standing for a plant container, ornament or sculpture. Alternatively, add areas of other natural materials, such as a cluster of boulders interspersed with plants; well-weathered timber or railroad ties (railway sleepers) sunk into the grass; perhaps a small beach of pebbles running down into the water. If you do not have the time and patience to sow seed and wait for the grass to grow, turfs create the perfect instant effect. Ideally, you should use the turfs you have saved from your pool excavation, provided you lifted and rolled them carefully. You can also buy them commercially. Buy good-quality turfs and be sure to keep them well watered until you are ready to use them.

Above: Timber decking is an excellent and stylish companion for large pools, where it can be used to create simple platform areas, jetties, bridges and walkways. By overhanging the water, a deck not only provides the opportunity to observe fish and plants at close quarters, but also makes the pool look larger than it really is. Timber decking combines well with other materials and because it can be built to any size and shape, the design possibilities are endless.

Left: A turf edging instantly gives a completely natural look to a pool and is easy to lay. The pool liner can be tucked beneath the soil and turfs to keep it firmly anchored.

Use a wood preservative that will not harm pond life.

Left: *Unless you want to create a natural sloping beach effect running into the pool, an edging of pebbles or small stones needs to be contained by wooden battens to prevent the stones spilling into the water. Use only washed stone to reduce the risk of introducing dirt or debris into the pool.*

Use the larger grade of chips rather than the finer composted type.

Left: *Bark chips can make an attractive edging alternative in an informal garden or woodland-type setting. Again, a wooden batten is useful to prevent the chips floating off into the water.*

Timber decking

Timber decking can be a quick and inexpensive alternative for pool edging. Whether raised feet or inches from the ground, it looks extremely stylish, yet is relatively easy to construct and flexible enough to create a wide range of effects. It can also be extremely useful for solving practical problems such as levelling a sloping or uneven site where building a retaining wall and backfilling would make a paved patio too expensive. Decking is also useful for linking features together, or converting a raised pool into a sunken one. The timber most commonly used for decking is a good water-repellent hardwood such as teak or oak, or one of the less expensive African hardwoods. This will require a couple of coats of preservative after installation, then an extra coat every spring or fall.

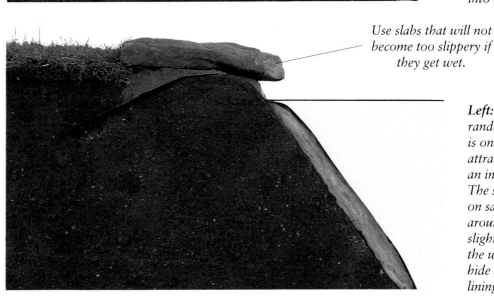

Use slabs that will not become too slippery if they get wet.

Left: *Grass with random stone slabs is one of the most attractive options for an informal pool. The slabs can be set on sand at intervals around the edge, slightly overlapping the water to help hide and anchor the lining material.*

Edging with slabs and bricks

Unit paving - that is, bricks, slabs, stone setts and stones, as opposed to continuous, poured concrete - is perfect for all but the most informal pool. It provides a neat and attractive finish that remains dry and practical underfoot, and which can be satisfactorily coordinated with, or matched to, other garden features. It easily disguises the pool edges and is perfect for weighting down or hiding those liner edges. Even better, it offers an infinite variety of creative possibilities, from mixing materials to laying them in unusual patterns, or even growing creeping plants in the cracks between them. You can use just a few slabs as a pool edging or extend the plan to create a full-scale patio or seating and eating area. Bricks and pavers come in a wide variety of colors, finishes, shapes and sizes, and some are designed to interlock and create sophisticated designs. Make sure that your chosen paving is frost and rain proof. Bricks are prone to splitting or flaking, so only use good-quality paving bricks. Thorough preparation of the ground is also essential for success. The foundations must be stable - not damp and boggy - even good friable soil is too crumbly. Rocky hardcore is far better and this can be used to backfill wherever you have had to excavate unsuitable soil. Remember that the finished level is crucial, so measure the depth of layers carefully.

Cement

Sand

Hardcore

The bricks slope slightly away from the water to prevent run-off into the pool.

Left: A brick edging needs good foundations: a 6in(15cm) layer of hardcore, 1in(2.5cm) of sand and 1in (2.5cm) of cement. By overlapping the edge of the pool slightly, the liner is completely concealed for a neat finish.

Cement

Sand

Hardcore

Check that slabs are level at every stage using a spirit level. Make sure that the total paved area slopes slightly backwards away from the water.

Left: *Paving slabs have a larger surface area to spread the weight of the people walking on them. They need only a 3in(7.5cm) layer of hardcore to give some substance to a damp or too crumbly soil base.*

The lawn edge here echoes the informal style of the pool and provides a smooth transition to the rest of the garden.

Above: *This random arrangement of broken flagstones not only conceals the liner but also creates a delightfully informal, yet practical, hard surface around this small garden pool.*

25

A pebble beach

A pebble beach makes an attractive informal edge for a natural effect pond or an oriental-style pool, and is also a good choice if you are planning a wildlife water garden, as birds and small mammals need a sloping edge to approach the water safely. Pebbles here will protect the liner from damage and maintain an attractive appearance. A grassy bank would quickly become a muddy quagmire under the onslaught of tiny feet. The pebbles must be smooth to prevent them damaging the liner and these are available graded into different sizes. When you excavate the pool, gently shape one side or a small area into a sloping bank - there is no need to install a beach all the way round the pool. Visually, an area of bank looks more attractive and provides the opportunity to incorporate a marginal shelf for growing an interesting range of water-loving plants. When you calculate your liner, allow extra width so that you can run it a good way up the slope. Anchor the end of the liner with soil, slabs or boulders, depending on the effect you are aiming for. Try to link the pebbles to the immediate surrounding area, either by running them up to a small bog garden for a totally natural effect or by inserting pebble sections into a paved area in a more formal design. Run the pebbles right down into the water for the most natural look.

Right: Boulders and pebbles are ideally suited to an informal area, the banks softened by hostas and other striking marginal plants. Take care when positioning heavy stones.

Left: Pebbled shallows create their own small feature area at the corner of a much larger pool. You can buy a wide range of pebbles, cobbles and boulders in various sizes and colors. Wash them thoroughly before use.

Right: *A carefully constructed pebble edging blends the formal with the informal in this charming patio pool with its millstone fountain.*

Below: *An area of rough stones is the perfect maintenance-free setting for a novel poolside sculpture, and fully complements both the water and the lush planting scheme around it.*

Setting up a water pump

If you have sufficient depth of water, a submersible pump is a neat way to run some kind of moving water feature, such as a fountain or waterfall. The pump remains submerged below the water level, making it easier to keep both the pump and pipework concealed. Submersibles are also easier to maintain and more economical to run than surface-mounted pumps. It is very important to calculate accurately the size of pump you need or the results may be very disappointing, especially if you are hoping to run more than one feature from the same pump using a T-piece in the outlet pipe. As the head of water increases, so the output will decrease; the length of pipe, its bore and the number of bends will also affect performance. It is not a good idea to run your pump at full capacity all the time, so it is better to buy a model slightly larger than your needs. Installing the pump is simple enough, providing it is close to a convenient outdoor electrical point. This supply should only be installed by a qualified electrician.

Flow rate and head

When you start to look for a suitable water pump for your pool you will see that the specifications mention flow rate per hour and maximum head of water. Bear in mind that the widest bore tubing that you can fit to the pump will help you achieve the optimum flow rate. 'Head' also reflects the power of the pump but in terms of the height the water can be pumped to in relation to the water level in the pool. Often, the flow rate is quoted at various heads.

You can connect this foam filter directly to the pump or at the end of a plastic tube.

Geyser fountain head

Bell fountain head

Extension tube

This part of the pump casing houses a block of plastic filter foam.

These adapters allow you to connect tubing of various diameters.

This is the electric motor that drives a spinning impeller to draw in water.

Water flow control

These are two samples of clear plastic tubing that will fit this pump. Black tubing is also sold for water pumps.

Use this cap to blank off the outlet.

This T-piece allows you to divert water into two outlets.

This fountain head produces a three-tier spray of jets.

This head produces two tiers of higher jets.

Internal diameter of 25mm(1in).

Internal diameter of 19mm(0.75in).

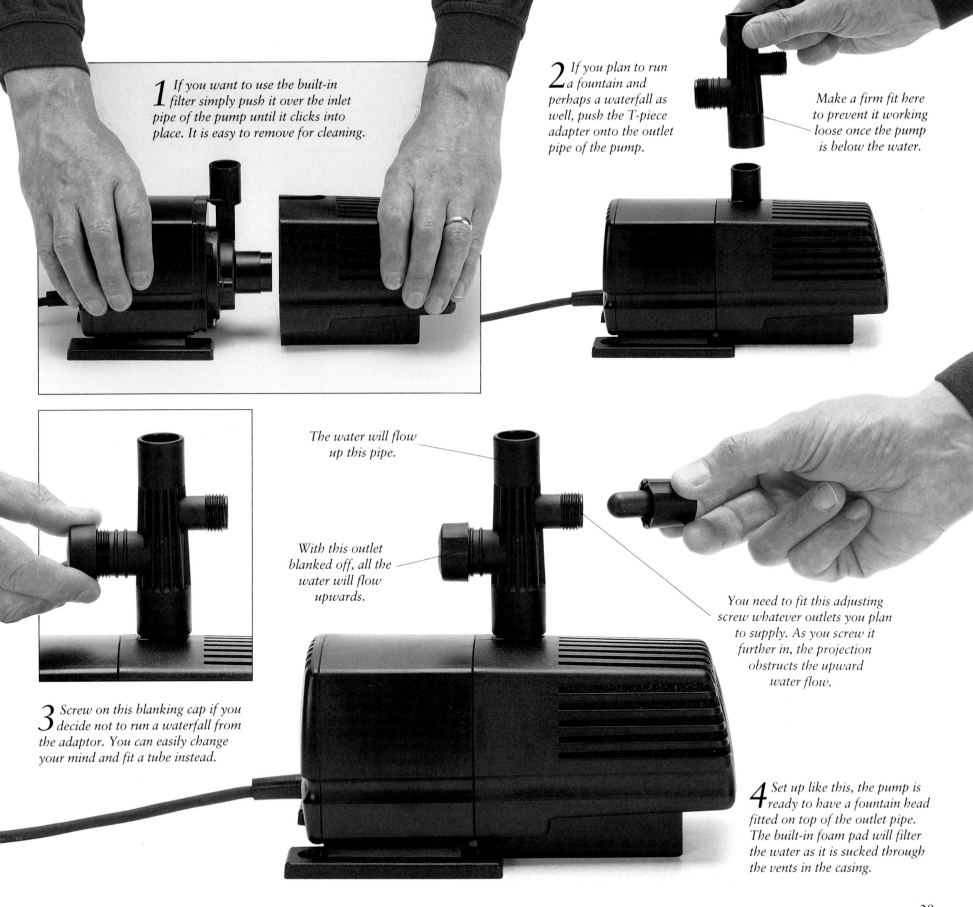

1 *If you want to use the built-in filter simply push it over the inlet pipe of the pump until it clicks into place. It is easy to remove for cleaning.*

2 *If you plan to run a fountain and perhaps a waterfall as well, push the T-piece adapter onto the outlet pipe of the pump.*

Make a firm fit here to prevent it working loose once the pump is below the water.

The water will flow up this pipe.

With this outlet blanked off, all the water will flow upwards.

You need to fit this adjusting screw whatever outlets you plan to supply. As you screw it further in, the projection obstructs the upward water flow.

3 *Screw on this blanking cap if you decide not to run a waterfall from the adaptor. You can easily change your mind and fit a tube instead.*

4 *Set up like this, the pump is ready to have a fountain head fitted on top of the outlet pipe. The built-in foam pad will filter the water as it is sucked through the vents in the casing.*

29

Installing a fountain

The splash and glitter of a fountain or water spout add excitement and pleasure to the smallest pool. Once you have put in the pump, installation could not be simpler; all you need is a fountain nozzle or jet, a length of plastic tubing and jubilee clips to connect them. Nozzles and jets come in a wide choice of types producing different effects, from tall plumes and multiple spray sequences, to a small bell or dome suitable for smaller pools. The mechanism might be hidden by an ornamental device, such as a human figure, a dolphin or other animal; or be skillfully incorporated into a classical or abstract sculpture. Some fountains come complete with lights and even music choreographed to the spray sequence. If you only have a tiny patio, or you have young children, you might prefer the option of a concealed reservoir where the water is recycled through a wall spout (via an old tap, a lion's head, a sculpted face or whatever you choose) into a small basin; or you could allow it to bubble over a bed of pebbles. There is something to suit everyone's taste, and style and size of garden.

Below: The fountain head with three circles of holes produces a three-tier pattern with a wide spread of water. Make sure the pool is large enough to catch the spray.

Right: Once you have fitted the T-piece into the top outlet of the pump, simply select the type of fountain head you wish to use. Most pumps are supplied with a choice of two spray patterns.

Below: This is the simplest way to provide a fountain. The submersible pump draws in water and forces it through the fountain head.

For best results, position the spray fountain head just above water level.

Control the height of the fountain by adjusting this water flow regulator.

Raise the pump on bricks to bring the fountain head to the correct level. This also helps to prevent the pump sucking in debris at the bottom of the pool.

Above: *The fountain head with two circles of holes produces a taller, two-tier pattern of water droplets.*

1 For a geyser fountain, first fit the extension tube onto the T-piece. This will raise the head well above the water level.

Air drawn in through these holes creates a frothy flow of water.

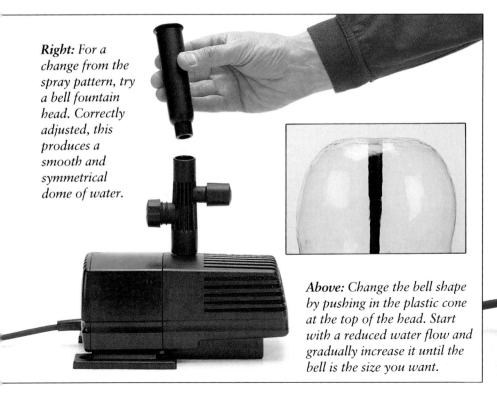

Right: *For a change from the spray pattern, try a bell fountain head. Correctly adjusted, this produces a smooth and symmetrical dome of water.*

Above: *Change the bell shape by pushing in the plastic cone at the top of the head. Start with a reduced water flow and gradually increase it until the bell is the size you want.*

2 Push the geyser head firmly onto the extension tube. You can alter the angle of the head to create different water flow patterns.

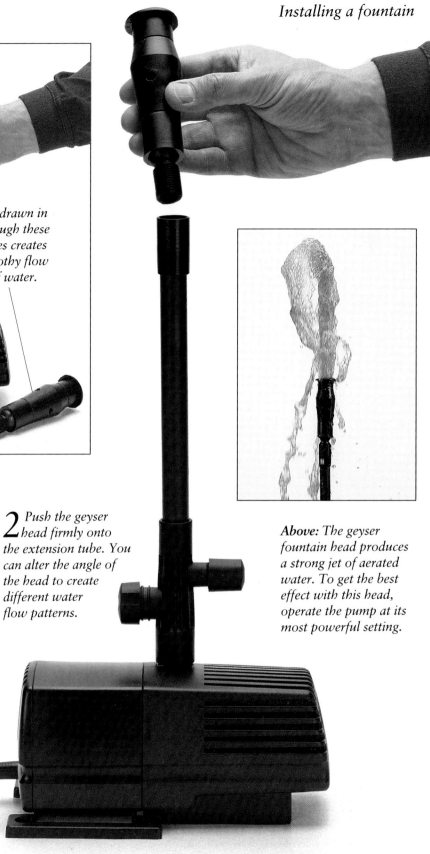

Above: *The geyser fountain head produces a strong jet of aerated water. To get the best effect with this head, operate the pump at its most powerful setting.*

Adding a waterfall

A waterfall or cascade is an excellent way to add movement - and, if necessary, height - to your garden scheme. It need not be large and, indeed, too tall a waterfall would require a tremendous volume of water and a very powerful pump to keep it circulating. Even a trickle from one formal patio pool into another slightly below it, makes a delightful feature. A rocky waterfall cascading over boulders into an informal pond is the perfect backdrop and a useful device to utilize waste stone and soil from your pool excavations. You will need a pump powerful enough to cope with the volume of water and the height of the falls; if you have already installed one of the larger types to run a fountain or other moving water feature, it may be possible to employ the pump to run both features by adding a T-piece to the outlet pipe. Your pump stockist should be able to advise you on the size and type of pump. If the waterfall is a big one, you may also need a top-up tank to maintain a large enough water supply. You can buy preformed fiberglass waterfalls that you can conceal behind boulders and plants to create the impression of a series of cascades.

Here the tubing has been left exposed to show where it runs. In your garden you can hide the tubing so that the water appears to spring from the stones.

Waterfall only

If you just want to run a waterfall, simply connect a suitable length of plastic tubing directly to the outlet of a submersible pump (as here) and direct the water flow as you wish.

The maximum size of the fountain depends on the height of the waterfall and the length of tubing involved.

Above: *An informal style cascade built up from slabs of stone needs a liner beneath it to prevent the water soaking into the surrounding soil.*

Left: *In this setup a submersible pump supplies water to a spray fountain and a waterfall. Make sure that the pump you choose can power both outlets.*

1 An 'add-on' foam filter can improve water quality, especially where you have fish in the pool. To fit it directly to the pump take out the central pipe connecter.

The foam not only strains out particles but also harbours bacteria to break down biological wastes.

2 Push the filter firmly onto the inlet pipe of the pump. The filter is easy to take off and pull apart for regular cleaning.

You can connect the foam filter to the pump with plastic tubing if you want to position them separately.

Setting up a pump for fountain and waterfall

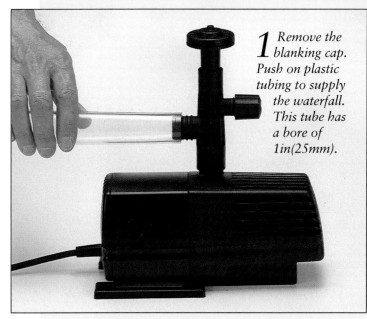

1 Remove the blanking cap. Push on plastic tubing to supply the waterfall. This tube has a bore of 1in(25mm).

2 Use the adjuster to control the flow of water. Fully screwed in, all the water will go to the waterfall; fully out will split the flow both ways.

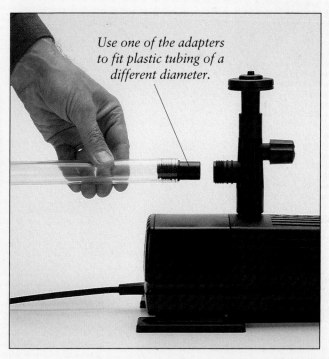

Use one of the adapters to fit plastic tubing of a different diameter.

33

Installing a water filter

A healthy pond relies on the correct biological balance between plants and animal life to keep unwelcome toxins and algae build-up to a minimum. In a large natural pool, nature makes its own adjustments and providing you keep rampant plants in check, you should not have any problems with green scummy water or waste materials from fish. However, in smaller pools with synthetic linings, you may need to install a water filter. This will circulate the water and keep it well-aerated and is a practical and economic consideration for small ponds. There are two main types of filter: you can recycle the water through an external system, which can be run off an existing pump, or you can install a sump at the bottom of the pool that filters the water through sand and stones or gravel via a separate pump. This usually incorporates a gauze filter pad that can be removed for cleaning. The simple filter system featured here will strain out particles of debris and suspended algae and will also reduce the levels of toxic wastes.

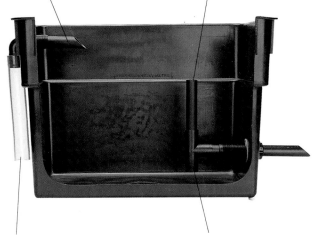

Water enters the filter here.

Water overflows through this tube if the filter floods.

Water pumped from the pool.

Water fills the bottom part of the filter and flows out here.

1 With the side cut away you can see how the pipework is arranged inside this typical biological filter suitable for small ponds up to 600 gallons (2,300 liters) in capacity.

These provide a large surface area for beneficial bacteria to colonize.

2 The bottom of the tank is filled with a biological filter medium. Here this consists of plastic corrugated pipe sections. These are inert and do not affect the water chemistry.

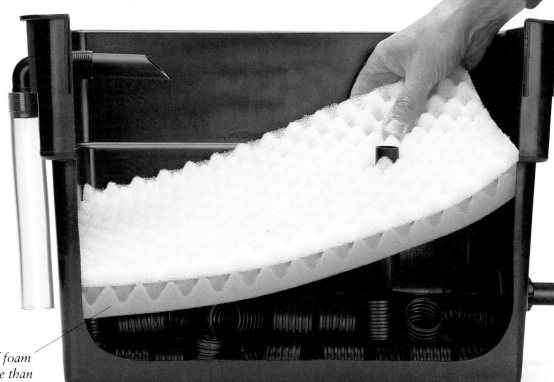

3 Two layers of plastic foam cover the filter medium. These strain out any debris in the water flowing from the pond.

The top layer of foam is a coarser grade than the lower one.

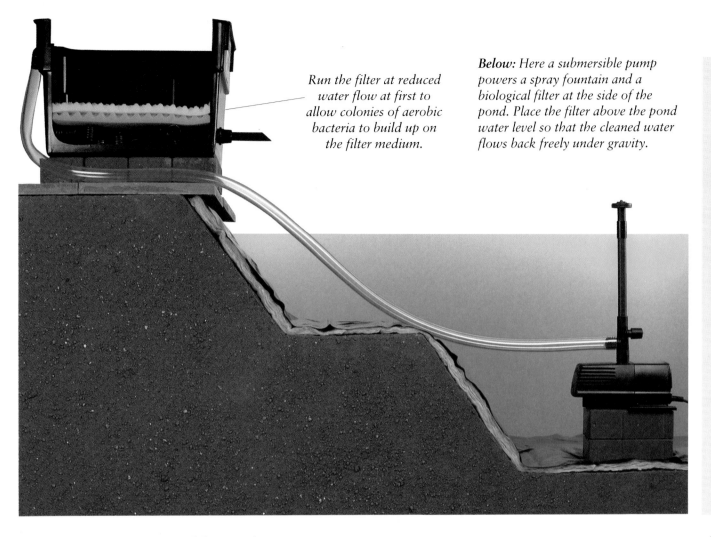

Run the filter at reduced water flow at first to allow colonies of aerobic bacteria to build up on the filter medium.

Below: *Here a submersible pump powers a spray fountain and a biological filter at the side of the pond. Place the filter above the pond water level so that the cleaned water flows back freely under gravity.*

How a biofilter cleans the water

A biological filter is so-called because it uses the biological processes of naturally occurring bacteria to clean the water of harmful biochemicals. The streams, rivers, lakes and seas of the world abound in bacteria. Some need oxygen to flourish and are therefore called aerobic bacteria. Among these are two groups that break down animal wastes into less harmful substances. The first group go to work on the highly toxic ammonia that animals excrete. They break this down to nitrites. Unfortunately, nitrites are also dangerously poisonous to most water creatures, even in low concentrations. Thankfully, the second group of aerobic bacteria break nitrites down to nitrates, which are much less toxic and are absorbed by plants as food.

In use a lid covers the top.

You can clean the top layer of foam without disturbing the lower one and filter medium.

Below: *Goldfish are hardy and tolerant of a wide range of water conditions, but a biological filter will help to keep the pond clean and clear.*

4 The filter is now ready for use. Make sure that the coarse grade of foam forms the top layer. Place the filter on a firm, level surface.

Cleaned water returns to the pond by gravity.

Aquatic baskets, liners and soil

Water plants can be planted directly into the soil or mulch at the bottom of the pool or on the marginal shelf, and with a large natural pool or lake this is often the most practical option. However, with smaller pools, using special rot-proof plastic pots and containers makes the plants - and pond - much easier to handle. A wide range of containers is available, their sides perforated to keep the soil moist and aerated. Baskets tend to have a wide base to make them stable and are usually black, which makes them virtually invisible once they are in the water. Large-weave baskets need lining with hessian or woven plastic material to prevent the soil washing away, but the containers with a close-weave pattern do not need lining. The soil you use for aquatic plants should be a rich and heavy loam to ensure that it has plenty of nutrients and remains waterlogged. A clay soil has the right consistency, but is usually not rich enough. Sandy or chalky soils are too fine and will wash out of the containers. Make sure that any soil you use is free from chemicals or herbicides.

This large plastic bowl is ideal for the more vigorous water lilies.

This type of planting basket is fine for water lilies in the early stages. Tiny perforations eliminate the need for a hessian liner.

Most water lilies can be planted in low-sided plastic bowls such as this.

Louvered sides prevent the loss of soil into the water.

A stout plastic bowl is ideal for small and miniature water lilies.

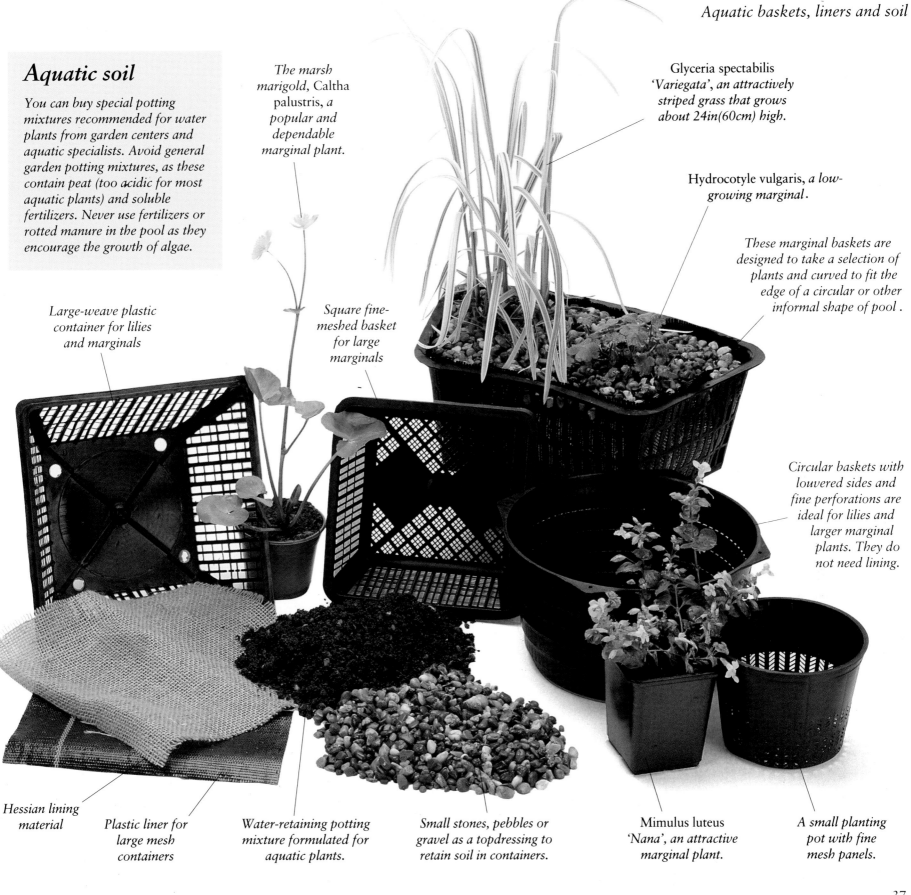

Aquatic soil

You can buy special potting mixtures recommended for water plants from garden centers and aquatic specialists. Avoid general garden potting mixtures, as these contain peat (too acidic for most aquatic plants) and soluble fertilizers. Never use fertilizers or rotted manure in the pool as they encourage the growth of algae.

The marsh marigold, Caltha palustris, *a popular and dependable marginal plant.*

Glyceria spectabilis *'Variegata', an attractively striped grass that grows about 24in(60cm) high.*

Hydrocotyle vulgaris, *a low-growing marginal.*

These marginal baskets are designed to take a selection of plants and curved to fit the edge of a circular or other informal shape of pool.

Large-weave plastic container for lilies and marginals

Square fine-meshed basket for large marginals

Circular baskets with louvered sides and fine perforations are ideal for lilies and larger marginal plants. They do not need lining.

Hessian lining material

Plastic liner for large mesh containers

Water-retaining potting mixture formulated for aquatic plants.

Small stones, pebbles or gravel as a topdressing to retain soil in containers.

Mimulus luteus *'Nana', an attractive marginal plant.*

A small planting pot with fine mesh panels.

Oxygenating plants

A selection of oxygenating plants is essential for the good health of your pool, especially if the pond is new. These are mostly submerged, or occasionally floating, species of water plants that use up waste nutrients in the water by means of their underwater foliage. This, and the fact that such plants grow prolifically, will quickly deprive bothersome algae of nutrients and minerals, and thus help to keep the water clean. Few oxygenators are as noticeably pretty as the water violet, *Hottonia palustris*, which produces a mass of pale mauve flowers above a dense underwater mat of fernlike foliage, but they generally do their job well, not only preventing green water and blanketweed, but also providing useful cover for pond insects and small fish. For the average pool, you will need about one oxygenating plant for every 2ft^2(five clumps per m^2) of surface area. Larger pools, over 150ft^2 (14m^2) can reduce that requirement to nearer one plant per 3ft^2(three bunches per m^2). Different species flourish at different times of year, so a selection of at least two or three species is the most successful way to beat murky water.

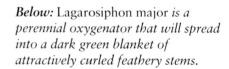

The tiny, semi-evergreen leaves of Lagarosiphon major *(also known as* Elodea crispa*) are clustered along each stem.*

Below: Lagarosiphon major *is a perennial oxygenator that will spread into a dark green blanket of attractively curled feathery stems.*

Left: Eleocharis acicularis, *or hairgrass, is an evergreen sedge that spreads prolifically by means of rhizomes to produce a dense mat of narrow green leaf spikes.*

Oxygenators

Callitriche hermaphroditica
(C. autumnalis)
Callitriche palustris (C. verna)
Ceratophyllum demersum
Crassula recurva
Eleocharis acicularis
Fontinalis antipyretica
Hottonia palustris
Lagarosiphon major
(Elodea crispa)
Myriophyllum proserpinacoides
Myriophyllum verticillatum
Potamogeton crispus
Ranunculus aquatilis

Below: Myriophyllum verticillatum, *whorled water milfoil, is a deciduous perennial that is usually grown for its unusual and highly eye-catching mass of bright green whorled leaves.*

Hottonia palustris, *or water violet, makes a clump of feathery, light green leaves, with tall spikes of pale lilac or white flowers in summer.*

Evergreen Fontinalis antipyretica *thrives in sun or semi-shade and prefers running water, such as a stream.*

Hardy Ceratophyllum demersum, *or hornwort, grows best in cool water, where it spreads to make a submerged mat of tiny dark green leaves.*

Ranunculus aquatilis, *the water buttercup, has bright green feathery foliage that can be invasive if not kept in check.*

39

1 One container with specially perforated sides will be sufficient for up to eight oxygenating plants, depending on the size of the pool. Use a trowel to fill it with potting mix.

Planting oxygenators

If you have a layer of soil at the bottom of your pond then oxygenators can be simply planted by weighting the stems with a small strip of lead or some similar device such as a small stone and dropping them into the water so that they become established. However, rooted types are best planted in plastic baskets, which makes them easier to maintain. Should the plant become too rampant, you can simply lift the basket and trim back the plant as required before replacing the container in the water.

Because oxygenators grow so prolifically, especially during the warmer months, they will need keeping in check, especially at the end of the summer. As a guide, you should not allow oxygenating plants to take up more than one third of the pool's volume or they will start to become as much of a problem as the hated green strands of blanketweed. In any case, it is a good idea to thin out your plants before they start dying back for the winter. Propagating oxygenating plants is equally straightforward. If you need more young, fresh plants, simply propagate them by dividing the bunches as shown on pages 62-63.

Use the aquatic soil specially formulated for water plants.

2 Fill the container almost to the rim. Use a dibble or your finger to make a sufficiently large planting hole for each plant.

3 Insert the first oxygenator into the planting hole and gently spread out the roots. Pack more potting mixture around the plant and firm it in carefully with your fingers.

4 Continue adding the rest of the plants you have chosen, planting them in the same way and positioning them evenly around the container.

Use clean washed gravel and avoid any minerals that might affect the water chemistry.

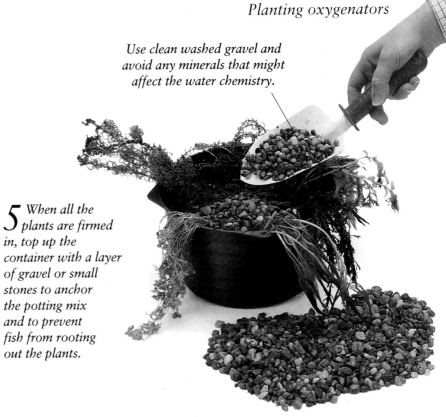

5 When all the plants are firmed in, top up the container with a layer of gravel or small stones to anchor the potting mix and to prevent fish from rooting out the plants.

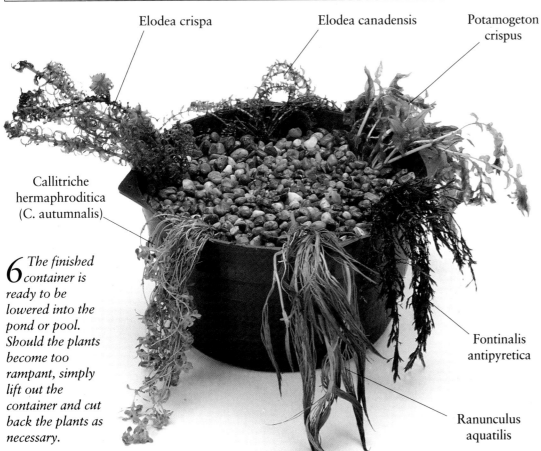

Elodea crispa

Elodea canadensis

Potamogeton crispus

Callitriche hermaphroditica (C. autumnalis)

6 The finished container is ready to be lowered into the pond or pool. Should the plants become too rampant, simply lift out the container and cut back the plants as necessary.

Fontinalis antipyretica

Ranunculus aquatilis

7 Once the plants are established in the basket, they will soon start to spread out below the surface of the water in the pond.

41

Floating plants

Floating plants are all those that are unrooted - that is, they float on, or just below, the surface of the water. Most of them require a water depth of about 12-36in(30-90cm) and are generally very easy to install, simply by resting the plant gently on the water surface and allowing it to find its own level. Naturally, this group includes a large number of oxygenators and, like oxygenators (see pages 38-39), floating plants will grow quickly within a single season. Consequently, you may need to take them out of the water to cut them back before they become too rampant.

Floating plants, such as the sturdy and beautiful water hyacinth *(Eichhornia crassipes)* or the tiny-leaved frogbit *(Hydrocharis morsus-ranae)* not only look good but also, unlike water lilies, grow quickly and establish useful cover within months of being put into the water. For this reason, it is not generally recommended that you put prolific floating plants into very large ponds. Unless you can devise some means of removing them, such plants could quickly become a pest and dominate the entire feature.

Above: Once it is established, perennial water hyacinth, Eichhornia crassipes, *produces beautiful lilac flower spikes each summer.*

A selection of floating plants

Azolla filiculoides
(Fairy moss)
Eichhornia crassipes
(Water hyacinth)
Hydrocharis morsus-ranae
(Frogbit)
Lemna trisulca
(Ivy-leaved duckweed)
Pistia stratiotes
(Water lettuce)
Riccia fluitans
(Crystalwort)
Stratiotes aloides
(Water soldier)
Trapa natans
(Water chestnut)
Utricularia vulgaris
(Bladderwort)

The water hyacinth, Eichhornia crassipes, *is a glossy evergreen or semi-evergreen water plant with attractive round-edged leaves.*

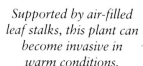

Supported by air-filled leaf stalks, this plant can become invasive in warm conditions.

Above: The ivy-leaved, or star duckweed, Lemna trisulca, *makes a mat of tiny green fronds, which are excellent for purifying the water.*

Above: Azolla filiculoides *comes from a family of floating water ferns that help to control pond algae. Reduce it using a net if it spreads too much.*

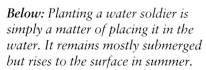

The floating annual, Trapa natans, or water chestnut, is grown for its attractive triangular leaves, white summer flowers and edible nuts.

Below: Planting a water soldier is simply a matter of placing it in the water. It remains mostly submerged but rises to the surface in summer.

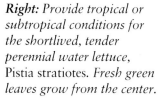

Above: The hardy water soldier Stratiotes aloides, *likes limestone waters and plenty of sun. In these conditions, it produces tiny white flowers in summer.*

Right: Provide tropical or subtropical conditions for the shortlived, tender perennial water lettuce, Pistia stratiotes. *Fresh green leaves grow from the center.*

43

Marginal plants

Varieties of Iris laevigata *include 'Regale', which has red blooms, and 'Snowdrift', which is white. 'Atropurpurea' has purple flowers.*

The plants that grow naturally along the banks and shallows of ponds and streams are among the most dramatic and beautiful species you could wish to feature in your garden. As a group, they include a wonderful variety of size, shape and color within the range of their foliage alone, while some have spectacular flowers, too, at certain times of the year. Even if your water feature is small, you will surely have space for one or two of these eye-catching plants, if only to feature as a focal point within your garden scheme. These plants are usually positioned on the marginal shelf, specially built just below the surface of the water, so that these mud-loving plants can keep their roots waterlogged. You can plant them directly onto the shelf in soil enriched with humus or pot them up into specially perforated plastic baskets for easy maintenance.

Buying plants

If you go to your local aquatic center at the beginning of the growing season, you will find rows of small plants, very few looking much like the exciting and dramatic foliage and flowering plants they will be once matured. Most of the plants featured on pages 44-55 and 64-79 have been photographed at this early stage and will provide a useful reference to help you choose relatively undeveloped specimens with confidence. Accompanying pictures show some of these and others in their mature form.

Right: Iris laevigata *will flourish in the shallows or in the moist soil of a bog garden or pool edge. The blooms appear above the spreading clump of smooth, green, spearlike leaves in early to midsummer.*

Iris pseudacorus
'Variegata' The
golden-yellow flowers
appear from early to
midsummer.

Iris ensata
(I. kaempferi)
'Variegata'

Scirpus
albescens

Above: Pontederia cordata, *or pickerel
weed, is popular as a marginal plant
both for its pretty blue-mauve flower
spikes and its lush, glossy green leaves.*

Ranunculus
flammula

Myriophyllum
proserpinacoides
*(Also featured as
an oxygenator)*

Cotula coronopifolia
'Brass Buttons'

45

Marginal plants

Marginal plants can add so much to the final appearance of your pond or pool. Apart from making a bit of a show, marginal plants help to soften the edges of a pool or stream; they might hide the liner and take away the rawness of a new excavation. Or the more dramatic species could add height and interest to an otherwise uninteresting garden. It is not a good idea to plant marginals all the way around the pool on the shelf provided, as this would totally obscure the pool itself and deny you access to the water's edge. It is more usual to plant up about one-third of the circumference as a kind of backdrop and gradually add more plants where you feel they might be needed. If they are positioned correctly, marginal plants not only provide visual interest but also give some shelter from prevailing winds and can be used to shade part of the water from midday sunshine. Minute forms of pondlife also enjoy the habitat created by the stems and roots submerged in the mud just below the water surface. Even young plants will lend an air of instant maturity and, in the rich, waterlogged soil, grow quickly to make it look as though the feature had always been there.

Below: In spring, the yellow skunk cabbage, Lysichiton americanus, is a striking sight alongside streams or pond. The shiny yellow arumlike flowers appear before the huge banana-shaped leaves, and give off a strange scent.

Iris laevigata *'Variegata'*

Myosotis scorpioides *'Mermaid'*

Left: *A dense growth of water forget-me-not,* Myosotis scorpioides (M. palustris), *brings summer color to the pond edge. This delightful plant will thrive in shallow water as a marginal or in moist soil as a bog plant.*

Above: *Juncus effusus, the soft rush, is one of the prettiest rushes. In summer, the mass of slender green stems is dotted with brown flower panicles.*

Lysichiton camtschatcensis. (*This and* L. americanus *will also flourish as bog plants in moist soil.*)

Mentha aquatica

Mimulus guttatus

Juncus effusus spiralis

Marginal plants

Even if yours is a modestly sized pond and you only need a few plants, you can have fun planning your marginal plants. The wide range of plant sizes and shapes offers the chance to contrast spiky reed and sword shapes with large shiny discs, delicate hearts, feathery ferns and fluttering plumes. There is a huge range of colors among the foliage of marginal plants, too: grays, greens, yellow, gold and silver can be coordinated and contrasted to make the perfect blend of form and hue. Flowers can be used for seasonal interest or to create a sudden burst of color as a focal point, and because they have an instant lush appeal, such plants can cunningly create the impression of water even if the pond or stream is 'dry'. Within an informal water garden you can achieve an interesting yet pleasant harmony; around the formal pool, the dramatic shapes and forms of marginal plants used in small groups have the perfect architectural impact.

Eleocharis palustris

Ranunculus grandiflora

Golden club (Orontium aquaticum) *will thrive in deeper water and can be lowered off the marginal shelf further out into the pond once established.*

Carex elata 'Aurea' (Bowles golden sedge)

Veronica beccabunga

Lobelia cardinalis 'Queen Victoria'

Right: Houttuynia cordata *'Plena'* has attractive heart-shaped, aromatic leaves and white spring flowers. It will thrive in shallow water or provide good ground cover in a damp semi-shaded position.

Houttuynia cordata *'Chameleon'*

Right: Golden club (Orontium aquaticum) produces these distinctive yellow flowers on pure white stems during spring. The robust leaves stand out of the water or lie on the surface.

Zantedeschia aethiopica

Preslia cervina (American water mint)

Sisyrinchium *'Boreale'*

Typha latifolia *'Variegata'*

Houttuynia cordata *'Plena'*

49

Marginal plants

The choice of shapes and colors among the flowers and foliage of marginal plants is so varied that planning your pool can be as much fun as interior decorating. Marginals with bright green feathery foliage contrast superbly with the shiny, arrowhead-shaped leaves of plants such as the Virginia arrow arum (*Peltandra virginica*), the beautiful heart-shaped leaves with purple undersides of *Ligularia dentata* 'Desdemona', the giant banana-like foliage of *Lysichiton americanus* (shown on page 46) or the elegant flat straps around the lovely blooms of iris. They all contrast perfectly with smaller-leaved marginals, such as *Geum rivale* and the marsh marigold (*Caltha palustris*). The tall spiky plants include grasses and sedges that prefer their roots to be waterlogged and are useful in natural water gardens because they bind together the banks of streams and ponds.

Virginia arrow arum (*Peltandra virginica*). The interesting arrow-shaped leaves will grow 12in(30cm) long and 6in(15cm) wide. It can become invasive so keep it in check.

Cotton grass (Eriophorum angustifolium)

Mimulus luteus 'Nana'. The flowers appear throughout the summer months.

Hemp agrimony (Eupatorium cannabinum)

Myrtle flag or sweet flag (Acorus calamus 'Variegatus')

Left: Eriophorum angustifolium, *sometimes called the common cotton grass, is distinguished by the soft silky white tufts that form on the tips of its slender green stems 12in(30cm) high.*

Left: Cyperus longus *(galingale). The dark green, grasslike, spreading foliage, which grows up to 5ft (1.5m) in height, bears attractive reddish-brown tufts in summer.*

Caltha palustris 'Alba' has rounded leaves and large buttercup flowers.

Galingale (Cyperus longus)

Carex pendula, a decorative water grass.

Geum rivale *makes clumps of green divided leaves and tiny orange flowers.*

Pennywort (Hydrocotyle vulgaris). *The shoots creep out onto the water*

Mimulus luteus *bears larger flowers than* M.l. 'Nana'.

Marginal plants

The smaller-leaved marginals might not be as dramatic as the giant moisture-loving plants, such as *Rheum* and *Gunnera* (featured on pages 78-79), but they have equal value within your water feature, especially if you plant them in massed groups of a single species for extra impact. This way, smaller leaves and flowers are not overlooked in larger pools. As a rule, smaller marginals grow quickly in damp mud, many of them providing quick ground cover to disguise and soften the banks and edges within a single season. Although smaller, the foliage is attractive and most produce pretty flowers, too, such as the spreading monkey musk, *Mimulus guttatus*. This hardy annual self-seeds readily to produce a carpet of small oval leaves along the edges of ponds and streams. In spring, you cannot beat the sight of bog arum, *Calla palustris*, with its white arumlike flowers and heart-shaped leaves. In summer, the yellow flowers of creeping Jenny *(Lysimachia nummularia)* appear among the dense, spreading, pale green carpets of foliage - quite different from the taller *Lysimachia thyrsiflora*.

Below: *In midsummer,* Mimulus guttatus *produces a mass of yellow orchidlike flowers with rust-colored blotches.*

The giant reedmace (Typha latifolia) produces distinctive soft brown pokers.

Typha stenophylla

Lysimachia thyrsiflora

Hypericum elodeoides

Left: Alisma plantago-aquatica, *the water plantain, is a deciduous marginal plant. Its bright green oval leaves are smothered in a web of delicate stems and tiny white flowers during the summer months.*

Sparganium erectum

Water plantain (Alisma plantago-aquatica)

Potentilla palustris

Euphorbia palustris

Above: Sagittaria sagittifolia, *the common arrowhead, grows happily in or near the water's edge and is prized for its striking arrow-shaped foliage. This hardy plant also produces three-petalled white flowers with purple centers in summer.*

Sagittaria sagittifolia 'Flore Pleno' (Japanese arrowhead)

Marginal plants

The environs of a successful water feature need careful planning if plants are to look natural together and the shapes and colors are to be harmonious. When choosing marginal and moisture-loving plants, your first consideration, after selecting the correct light or shade and soil requirements, must be height and size. Decide which vantage points the pond or pool will be viewed from and select your plants accordingly. Restrict taller, spiky plants to the back of the pond and use the rampant, ground-covering species to smother the banks or beds towards the front. Exercise this element of design control even when planning a slightly wild, informal type of pool, and allow access to the water by not planting all the way round. This is not purely for the purposes of plant maintenance, but also to allow you to enjoy plants and wildlife at closer quarters. You may have to keep some of the more prolific species in check to maintain the desired effect. Among your marginal plant selection, try to achieve a good contrast of shapes and shades using different foliage effects, as well as blooms. With marginal plants, that contrast can be quite dramatic, as many types in this group have strong architectural qualities. Add seasonal interest with plants that flower at different times of the year. There are even a few species that put on a display at the end of summer when their leaves change color or they produce interesting seedheads.

Right: The upright, cylindrical stems of bulrush *(Scirpus sp.)* growing in the water provide an attractive backdrop to the broad leaves of Hosta crispula *thriving on the damp pond edge.*

Right: Deciduous perennial Colocasia esculenta, *or taro, is grown for its bold, strongly marked foliage. It forms a close mound of pointed, heart-shaped dark green leaves with the veins sometimes picked out dramatically in white.*

Left: Typha minima, *is ideal for the shallow edges of smaller ponds. It has slender green foliage so fine it almost looks like grass, and bears distinctive brown pokers in late summer.*

The marsh marigold (Caltha palustris) is a must for every pond. It produces an abundant display of bright yellow flowers in early spring and summer. There is a white version ('Alba' - shown on page 51) and a yellow form with double flowers ('Flore Pleno').

Typha minima

Rumex
sanguineus

Glyceria maxima
'Variegata'

Zebra rush
(Scirpus zebrinus)

Saururus cernuus

Planting a marginal

Marginal plants will thrive with their roots submerged in water but their foliage must be free of the water surface. It is important to plant them quickly, so that their roots and stems are exposed for as short a time as possible, and you must plant them at exactly the same level as they were in the pot or nursery bed. Remove the plants carefully from their container, but not until you have everything ready to plant, otherwise the roots may suffer. If you are planting in a bog or marsh area (you can use many marginals as bog plants), all you do is simply dig a hole about four times the size of the rootball, water the plant well and lower it gently into the hole, making sure it is at the right level. Replace the soil (enriched with organic matter if necessary) and firm in the plant. If you have a 'natural' pond with soil submerged around the edges, you can plant directly on the marginal shelf by backfilling with a suitably rich, water-retaining soil. Hold the plants in place with large rocks or boulders. For pools with 'clean' marginal shelves you can use special containers that you can lower onto the shelf and lift out for easy maintenance. These containers are available in various sizes suited to single specimens or several plants together. Curved baskets are ideal for the marginal shelf around a circular pool.

1 Once you have assembled all the materials and plants you need, begin filling the marginal basket with moist aquatic potting soil.

2 Remove the marginal plant gently from its pot, taking care to support the stem loosely between your fingers.

Keep the plants moist and in their original pots until you use them.

Make sure that the topdressing of gravel is clean and washed.

3 Position the plants carefully in the container. Two or three plants of the same species will make a good display. Backfill and firm in.

4 Finish filling the container with aquatic soil and level the surface. Add a layer of gravel so that the potting mix does not float away.

5 The finished container is ready to be lowered onto the marginal shelf of the pond. When filled with soil, plants and gravel, it is quite heavy.

6 Holding the container firmly by the handles on both sides, lower it gently onto the marginal shelf without disturbing the water too much.

7 The marginal basket is in position on the shelf with the plants visible from the pool edge. It is easy to lift the container out for maintenance.

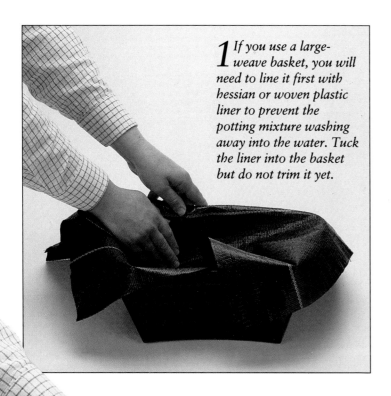

1 *If you use a large-weave basket, you will need to line it first with hessian or woven plastic liner to prevent the potting mixture washing away into the water. Tuck the liner into the basket but do not trim it yet.*

Planting a contour basket using a liner

Special planting baskets for use in pools come in a wide range of sizes and shapes to take one or several marginal or aquatic plants. Since you do not want to be fishing them in and out of the water too frequently, it makes sense to take the time and trouble to plant them up correctly in the first place. Baskets should only need lifting when plants have become too rampant and require thinning or replacing. When you have selected the correct sized basket, it may need lining to prevent the soil washing out through the perforations into the water. This also makes it easier to remove the plants should it be necessary at a later date. When it is finished, the container, complete with damp soil, plants and pebbles, will be heavy, so lower it with care; never drop it even a short distance or you will disturb the water and possibly damage your liner. Get into the water if necessary if you cannot reach comfortably by leaning over. It is important that baskets are positioned at the correct level for the plants' usual depth requirements. In deep water they may need propping up on bricks or blocks.

2 *Press the liner material lightly and evenly into the container. Now you can start filling the basket with a suitable aquatic potting mixture.*

This plastic lining material will allow water into the basket but will not rot away when immersed.

3 *Remove the plants from their pots and position them in the basket, making sure that they are at the correct planting depth and are standing upright. These are marginal plants.*

4 Carefully backfill and top up the basket with potting mixture, firming in the plants as you go.

5 Add a layer of small stones or gravel to keep the potting mixture in place once the container is submerged.

6 When the container is planted, trim away any excess liner using a pair of sharp scissors.

7 This is the finished container, lined and planted and ready to be lowered onto the marginal shelf.

Iris laevigata 'Variegata'

Zantedeschia aethiopica

1 *This aquatic plant has already started to produce roots from nodes along the stem and so is an ideal subject for propagation by taking cuttings.*

Propagating aquatic plants by cuttings

Spring is the best time to take cuttings of plants in the water garden, as they will have the growing season ahead of them to get established. The new plantlets can be grown on in nursery beds or tanks of waterlogged soil - marginal species can often be grown in damp soil and introduced gradually to increasingly deeper water as the foliage grows taller. You can swap new plants with friends as an inexpensive means of acquiring different varieties or use them in or around your own pool as required. Rampant water garden plants tend to grow loose and leggy after a while and it is a good idea to maintain a continuous program of propagating from existing plants each year. This way you can keep your display looking in peak condition at no extra cost. Studying your plant will usually tell you if it is suitable material for taking cuttings. With plants grown in damp conditions, you will often find tiny roots along the stem near a node or leaf joint and this will make your job even easier. Spring cuttings tend to be what are called soft stem cuttings - that is, non-flowering shoots cut just below a leaf node and the lower leaves removed. By removing several sections from a single shoot, you can create several new plants from one stem. Be sure to keep the cuttings misted until they have started new root growth. When they are fully established you can plant them out.

2 *Take hold of the fleshy stem at a point close to where a leaf node has started to make healthy root growth.*

3 *If you pinch sharply between finger and thumb, the required section of stem should come away in your hand.*

4 *Remove the leaves from the stem below the root growth. Again, remove the leaves by pinching them sharply and cleanly between finger and thumb.*

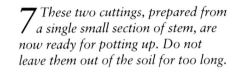

Make sure that the cuttings are not damaged or affected by disease or plant pests.

5 *Pinch off the top of the stem, too; this will give you another plant to propagate, even though there is no evidence yet of roots on this section.*

In moist conditions this cutting will soon produce new roots to support it.

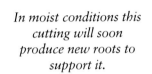

7 *These two cuttings, prepared from a single small section of stem, are now ready for potting up. Do not leave them out of the soil for too long.*

The small bundle of roots here will establish the new plant quickly.

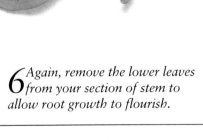

6 *Again, remove the lower leaves from your section of stem to allow root growth to flourish.*

8 *Gently insert the cuttings into small pots of damp potting mixture and firm in. Keep well watered until good leaf and root growth are under way and then transfer them to the water garden.*

1 *Start by filling sufficient small pots to hold your cuttings with a potting mixture recommended for moisture-loving plants.*

2 *Water the pots well until the potting mixture is soaked through. Standing the pots in a plastic tray helps to reduce and contain the mess.*

3 *Hold the plant loosely in one hand and gently tease apart the rootball with the other, taking care not to damage the roots or stems. Set aside each plantlet ready for potting up.*

Propagating aquatic plants by root division

Root division is one of the simplest forms of propagation and since its primary purpose is to reduce an over-large plant to more manageable proportions, it is good for reviving the original specimen, too. Again, spring is the best time to start digging up marginal or moisture-loving plants and splitting them up, giving new plants the summer months to establish new growth before they die back for the winter. The type of plants suitable for root division will be established hardy perennials that have obviously become overgrown. If you dig them up and examine them carefully, you can often see from the rootball that the plant is in fact several plants clustered together. Breaking or pulling them apart is a simple job, although tough roots may need to be cut with a sharp knife. The technique involved is exactly the same as you would use to split up land-based garden plants. Some water garden plants, such as iris, grow from thick rhizomatous roots that produce sucker shoots, and these are ideal for cutting into separate plants. (This technique is featured on page 17.) Other water plants have tuberous roots that need to be carefully divided into shooted sections.

Make sure that each plantlet has a healthy growth of roots and that the foliage is free from damage or disease.

4 *Several separate plantlets should naturally come away in your hand. Handle them very carefully.*

5 *Without crushing the stem, insert each plantlet in a prepared pot, allowing the roots plenty of room to spread themselves out.*

6 *Top up the pot with damp potting mix and firm it around the plant with your fingertips to ensure that the plant is straight and stable.*

Below: *The bright splashes of red and cream on the green leaves of this Houttuynia cordata 'Chameleon' make this a prized plant for adding welcome color to the water's edge.*

Below: *One single specimen, such as this Houttuynia, might yield as many as half a dozen new plants for the water garden. With care, each one will grow on strongly.*

Moisture-loving plants

Below: Japanese flag, Iris ensata (or I. kaempferi), is a beardless iris with large flowers, each measuring 3-6in (7.5-15cm) across. There is also an all-white form ('Alba') and one with variegated leaves (I. ensata 'Variegata').

There are many interesting plants that flourish in moist but well-drained soil and they look perfect when planted to create a lush profusion of flowers and foliage near, or leading away from, the pond edge. Some are marginal plants that will tolerate damp but not totally waterlogged conditions and these can be used in either position. Many are simply hardy garden perennials that you may already be familiar with from your herbaceous borders, and that prefer a moist, rich location. Others look the part but will actually tolerate drier conditions - at least on a temporary basis. This gives you plenty of scope to devise a suitable background planting plan for your particular pond or water feature, one that will blend readily into the rest of the garden or patio design.

Below: Day lilies, Hemerocallis, bear beautiful but brief-lived lilylike flowers among deep green straplike foliage. This one is 'Pink Damask'.

Left: *Perennial* Anemone rivularis *is a good ground cover plant in damp areas. Its deeply divided green leaves are studded with white flowers with yellow centers in late spring and early summer. This plant will flourish in an area with damp soil and grow to a height of about 24in(60cm).*

Iris sibirica
'*Sparkling Rose*'

Primula x '*Geisha Girl*'

Cowslip
(Primula veris)

Day lily
(Hemerocallis)

Primrose
(Primula vulgaris)

Moisture-loving plants

Moisture-loving plants are ideal for maintaining that poolside look, where there may not be a natural wet edge - in patio gardens, for example, or where the pond has a butyl or concrete liner. Because most of them grow prolifically given the right conditions, and as the majority have striking flowers or foliage (or both), they are an eye-catching part of the feature and have a wonderful softening effect on pond or stream edges, even in a patio location. To create the right effect around a small patio pond surrounded by paving, you can plant several of these lush species in pots or containers and position them in close groups near the water. Keep the containers well watered and mulch them in dry weather. Where you do have access to soil or planting beds, it helps to make sure that the soil is rich in humus to keep it damp and to mulch well to prevent moisture loss. If you cannot keep the soil damp, you will have to choose those plants that tolerate drier conditions or create a bog or marsh area as described on pages 80-83.

Right: *During early summer, hardy* Primula japonica *produces tall stems of dark red flowers rising above dense clumps of pale green leaves.*

Heuchera 'Pewter Moon'

Primula denticulata

Geranium sanguineum

Primula denticulata

Left: *The globeflower,* Trollius x cultorum *'Canary Bird', with its dazzling display of bright yellow blooms, is one of the heralds of spring along streams and ponds.*

Right: *The tubular red flowers and fleshy green foliage of* Primula pulverulenta *'Inverewe' make a fine upright display in early summer.*

Trollius chinensis *'Golden Queen'*

Primula vulgaris flore-plena *'Ken Dearman'*

Moisture-loving plants

Since the range of plants included under the description 'moisture-loving' is so vast, it pays to check exactly which conditions each plant prefers, so that you are sure of putting it in the right place within your overall planting scheme. Some of the moisture-lovers will thrive equally well on the marginal shelf; other species - or even a variety of species - will not survive for long if the soil is a little too waterlogged. There are plants that can surprise you; artemisias, for example, generally prefer drier conditions, but *Artemisia lactiflora* is a native of meadowland and stream valleys and will do well in damp soil. Check, too, whether your chosen plant prefers a sunny or shady position, as this can also drastically affect its chances of success. Some, such as *Lysichiton* and *Hemerocallis* will tolerate both sunshine and some shade.

These terminal flowerheads are borne on stems that reach up to 7ft (2.1m) tall.

Above: Lobelia cardinalis *is prized for its deep red flower spikes and bronze foliage, which make such an excellent contrast to the lusher, green foliage of most moisture-loving plants.*

Left: Joe Pye Weed, Eupatorium purpureum, *is a useful, tall perennial that produces heads of pink flowers during late summer and early fall.*

68

Aquilegia
'Nora Barton'

Aquilegia alpina

Above: *Astilbes make an excellent
display of feathery plumes along pond
margins and boggy borders. Like
Astilbe x ardensii shown here, they
appreciate a little shade.*

Astilbe
'Straussenfeder'

Above: *With its fluffy heads of
creamy-white flowers in midsummer,
meadowsweet, Filipendula ulmaria,
is a favorite choice for informal pool
edges and bog gardens.*

Ligularia dentata
'Desdemona'. *This
will also thrive as a
marginal plant.*

Achillea millefolium
'Cerise Queen'

Lysimachia
nummularia
'Aurea'. *Also fine
as a marginal.*

Moisture-loving plants

Plants that will tolerate a moist, waterlogged soil can be successfully planted close by the pool edge or in a specially created bog garden. A bog or marsh area might be used as a complementary extension of the pond edges or, if you have no other kind of water in the garden, installed as a separate feature in order to grow a selection of these often dramatically lush plants. You might consider the prolific umbrella plant, *Peltiphyllum peltatum*, whose large parasol leaves grow up to 12in(30cm) across. There is also a dwarf variety for smaller gardens. Most ferns will thrive in the moist soil of the shadier side of the pond or bog garden, while for a blaze of seasonal color there are many free-flowering sunlovers to choose from, including the stately purple loosestrife, *Lythrum salicaria*.

Above: *If pruned, the Siberian dogwood, Cornus alba 'Sibirica', produces a splendid display of bright red shoots in winter.*

Above: *The striking red foliage of Cornus alba 'Sibirica' turns deep green in late spring, when creamy-white flowers appear.*

Left: *In contrast to the larger-leaved, lusher water plants,* Aruncus dioicus 'Glasnevin' *has more delicate fernlike foliage and plumes of attractive white flowers during the summer months.*

Right: *Ligularia przewalskii 'The Rocket' produces loose clumps of striking yellow flower spikes that provide late summer interest around the margins of the water garden.*

Left: *The summer snowflake,* Leucojum aestivum, *actually flowers in spring, when it makes a welcome display of delicate white flowers and dark green stems.*

Geranium phaeum

Ligularia przewalskii *'The Rocket'*

Primula rosea

Aquilegia longissima *McKana hybrid*

Aquilegia vulgaris *(variegated form)*

71

Moisture-loving plants

If you can provide a rich, damp but well-drained soil, there are many
delightful plants to choose from. Consider the pretty meadow flowers for
the sunny sites, and woodland beauties for shady corners. For foliage
interest, most ferns prefer a moist shady site and many hostas grow well in
partial shade. Use the sun-lovers to make a brilliant border to be reflected
in the water surface on bright days. The planting scheme can lead off into
the rest of the garden and drier flower beds beyond. Blend astilbe's feathery
plumes with the elegant iris, the butter-yellow, ball-like blooms of the
globeflower, *Trollius*, (shown on page 67) or with a selection of the many
spring and summer-flowering primulas, with their jewel-like colors and
thick velvet foliage. For a superb display later in the year, the kaffir lily,
Schizostylis, produces a show of freesia-like blooms in shades of red, white
and pink. The small blue flowers of *Sisyrinchium bellum* also last until fall.

Above: *Sometimes called cuckoo
flower or lady's smock, pretty*
Cardamine pratensis *makes a show of
delicate lilac flowers in spring.*

Left: *Providing you can keep
the slugs and snails at bay,
hostas thrive in moist shady
conditions and make a
superb display of thick
quilted foliage. Hosta
sieboldiana, shown here, is
one of the largest, with
generous heart-shaped leaves
with an almost blue tinge.*

Left *Hostas can offer many interesting color and pattern variations. Hosta fortunei aureomarginata, as its scientific name reflects, has golden yellow borders to thick green leaves.*

Iris hoogiana 'Hula Doll'

Iris innominata 'Irish Doll'

Iris innominata 'Jack o' Hearts'

Hosta 'Sun Power'

Sisyrinchium bellum

Lamium maculatum 'White Nancy'

73

Moisture-loving plants

Moisture-loving plants that prefer, or at least will tolerate, a little shade are invaluable for those shady areas around the pool or in the corner of the patio where other plants will not thrive. It is worth seeking out a few such species to avoid ugly gaps or sickly specimens of plants that would rather be out in the sun. Look out for woodland plants, such as *Astilbe chinensis* 'Pumila' that make good ground cover and produce rose-colored flower spikes in summer in moist, shady places. Bistort, *Polygonum bistorta* 'Superbum', will tolerate dense shade and grow prolifically, making a carpet of tall leaves and pokers of tiny pink flowers by early summer. Many have striking foliage, such as the variegated figwort, *Scrophularia auriculata* 'Variegata', with tall green leaves splashed with cream.

Above: Clump-forming knotweed, Polygonum amplexicaule *'Atrosanguineum', produces a blaze of tiny red flower spikes in late summer.*

Left: The water figwort, Scrophularia auriculata *'Variegata', forms clumps of cream-splashed green foliage that is useful for lighting up damp areas in semi-shade.*

Right: The giant reed, Arundo donax, *makes an elegant clump of tall, flaglike foliage up to 20ft(6m) tall in moist soil. The smaller variety 'Versicolor' has creamy-white stripes along the leaves.*

Left: *Bistort*, Polygonum bistorta *'Superbum', grows well in damp conditions and makes a mass of pale pink pokers that are popular with bees throughout the summer.*

Right: *Parnassia palustris thrives in wet soil and full sun, producing beautiful upturned white saucers in late spring and early summer.*

Bergenia crassifolia

Achillea ptarmica 'The Pearl'

Schizostylis coccinea major

Astrantia major

Alchemilla mollis

Dactylorhiza maculata

Moisture-loving plants

In areas near or around the water feature, where the soil may occasionally dry out, there are a few lush-looking plants that prefer a moist position, but will usefully tolerate temporarily dry conditions. Save these for those spots where you know you will not be able to maintain permanently damp soil. These might be the outer limits of your poolside planting scheme or the pots and planting beds of a patio water garden. *Hemerocallis*, the day lily, (see page 64) is very adaptable and will withstand quite dry conditions. Hostas are also more tolerant of drier soils than you might expect, providing they have some shade to compensate for lack of moisture in the ground. For areas that stay moist, the ferns are an ideal group to investigate.

Below: *White-striped gardener's garters, Phalaris arundinacea 'Picta', grows prolifically in damp soil.*

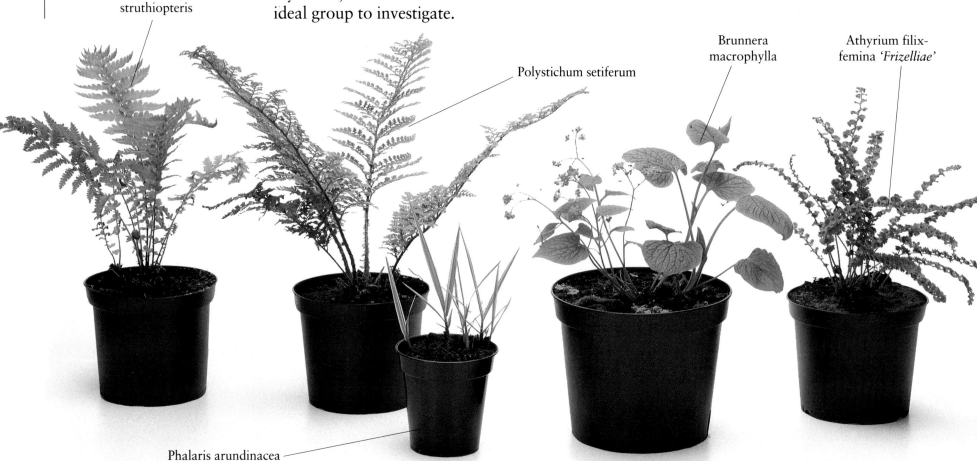

Matteuccia struthiopteris

Polystichum setiferum

Brunnera macrophylla

Athyrium filix-femina *'Frizelliae'*

Phalaris arundinacea

Left: *The royal fern,* Osmunda regalis, *prefers a waterlogged soil but will tolerate sun and shade. It produces a magnificent display of fronds up to 6ft(1.8m) and 3ft(90cm) across.*

Right: *The unfurling fronds of the striking ostrich fern* (Matteuccia struthiopteris) *create interesting patterns as they catch the light. This native of marshy areas will provide a splendid display in a bog garden.*

Geum borisii

Geum chiloense 'Mrs J. Bradshaw'

Asplenium scolopendrium 'Marginatum'

Sensitive fern (Onoclea sensibilis)

Dryopteris filix-mas 'Crispa Cristata'

Moisture-loving plants

One of the most exciting aspects of having the opportunity to grow moisture-loving plants is the wonderful selection of dramatic large-leaved species that thrive in the naturally damp conditions. The lush effect of even one of these plants can quickly and effectively fill a corner, make a focal point, or help to create the impression of a jungle of foliage. They contrast perfectly with other, smaller marginal plants, such as iris or primulas. There are plants such as the ornamental rhubarb, *Rheum palmatum*, for example, with spectacular bright green leaves that grow up to 36in(90cm) across. The plant might reach 6ft(1.8m) tall. Equally stunning is *Gunnera manicata*, the largest-leaved plant that you can grow in garden conditions, with each cut-edged leaf capable of growing up to 5ft(1.5m) across. Both these outsize plants will grow in shade or sun. The many other plants with large but perhaps not quite as dramatic foliage include the Japanese butterbur, *Petasites japonicus*.

Gunnera manicata. *A superb architectural plant for a spacious location. Notice the flower spike among the central leaves.*

Left: Rodgersia pinnata *'Superba' is popular along the banks of lakes and pools, as much for its fine divided foliage, often tinged with bronze, as for the mass of starry pink flower spikes it produces in midsummer.*

Ornamental rhubarb
(Rheum palmatum)

These magnificent five-lobed leaves create a stunning effect in the garden. Small white flowers appear in early summer borne on broad panicles.

Above: Glossy green Rheum alexandrae *hides its cream flower spikes behind large greenish-white bracts in early summer. These later turn red.*

Right: *Another moisture-loving plant with both attractive leaves and flowers is* Cimicifuga racemosa. *The leaves are deeply divided and bright green, the summer flowers a mass of bold white pokers.*

Creating a bog garden or marsh area

1 *If there is not already a natural depression in the ground, begin by excavating the area to a depth of about 14in(35cm).*

2 *Roughly level the base of the hole and make sure there are no large stones or other sharp objects in the soil that might puncture the liner.*

3 *Spread the area with a large sheet of pond lining material. You can use butyl rubber or a less expensive PVC-based type of liner.*

To create a bog garden or marsh area you need to excavate the desired area to a depth of about 14in(35cm), cover it with a large sheet of punctured butyl or other pond lining material and fill it with water-soaked soil. Ideally, there should be water standing about 2in(5cm) on the top. It is important to keep the area poorly drained and to make allowances for fluctuations in the water level according to the differing levels of rainfall throughout the year. In a naturally boggy site this is not a problem, but where you have created the environment artificially, you will need some kind of overflow facilities. This is easily installed where the bog garden adjoins a pool area by providing a few holes (about 0.5in/1.25cm in diameter) in the dividing wall. For this two-way top-up drainage system to work, the bog area should represent no more than about ten to fifteen percent of the total surface area of the pond. If there is no pond next to the bog garden, then you can install overflow facilities into a nearby ditch. The easiest way to top up the moisture levels in a dry spell is to insert a length of punctured plastic pipe at the construction stage. If you conceal the exposed end of the pipe among the plants in the bog garden you can easily trickle in more water as and when required.

Right: *A bog or marsh area offers the chance to grow a selection of exciting marginal plants, such as hostas, iris, typha, mimulus, phalaris and violas.*

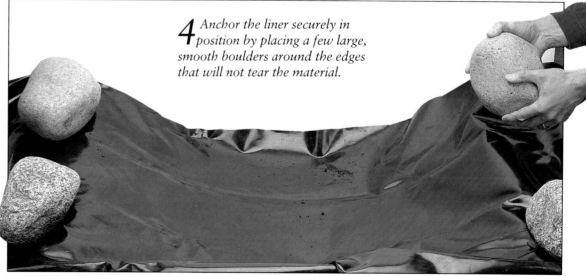

4 *Anchor the liner securely in position by placing a few large, smooth boulders around the edges that will not tear the material.*

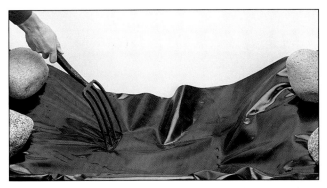

5 Puncture the bottom of the liner a couple of times with a garden fork, so that some of the water can escape later on.

6 Spread a layer of washed gravel over the lining at the bottom of the bog area. This will help the soil to retain moisture once it is established.

7 Lay a section of perforated pipe on the gravel in the bottom of the excavation. Allow the end of the pipe to extend beyond the bog garden area and conceal it in the undergrowth.

Make irrigation holes in the pipe 12in(30cm) apart.

8 With the irrigation pipe in place, fill the area to the original ground level with a rich, moisture-retaining aquatic planting mixture.

9 Soak the ground thoroughly, so that about 3in(7.5cm) of water remains standing on the top of the soil before you start putting in any plants.

Planting up the bog garden

1 When the soil is saturated with water, you can start to add a selection of suitable bog garden plants. There is plenty of choice.

2 Position the plants in the ground so that they are at the same depth as they were in their pots or nursery bed. Firm them in well.

Here we show how to plant up the bog garden created on pages 80-81. The beauty of creating a bog or marsh area in the garden is that it offers you the chance to grow a wider range of exciting marginal plants. Or you may welcome the chance to establish a rewarding water feature without the need for expensive excavation work. Ideally, the site should be sheltered from prevailing winds with a little, but not too much, shade. The most natural position is adjoining the banks of an informal pond or pool, but if you are planning an individual bog garden, then any slight depression or poorly drained area will make an ideal site. You should try to avoid positioning your bog garden too near any tree roots as they tend to drain moisture from the soil. If your garden is small or unsuitable, you can still enjoy a miniature bog garden created in an old stone sink or barrel, providing there are three or four drainage holes and a good layer of crocks in the bottom. You can grow one or two moisture-loving plants in each container as long as you keep the soil saturated; mulching with pebbles helps to reduce moisture loss. The containers can stand on the patio or in the garden; a series of tubs containing different plants and sunk to their rims in a bed of gravel looks particularly effective. Or arrange several old sinks on the patio at various levels.

3 Do not hesitate to arrange clumps of a single species, here Primula veris, to create an impact with more delicate-looking bog plants.

4 Some marginals, such as this hosta, offer wonderful shape and color possibilities simply in their foliage. Remember to protect these plants against the attentions of slugs and snails.

5 *Fill in any spaces between the new plants with washed pebbles to reduce moisture loss and create an attractive background.*

6 *In extremely dry conditions, you can easily top up the water level using the piece of pipe you inserted at the construction stage.*

7 *Aim for a variety of shape, size and color in your plants to produce an eye-catching display throughout the growing season.*

Lysimachia thyrsiflora

Astilbe

Lobelia cardinalis

Primula veris

Pipe left accessible for watering

Mimulus

Mimulus

Hosta

Small water lilies

Above: Nymphaea pygmaea 'Helvola'. *This delightful miniature variety bears canary-yellow, star-shaped flowers throughout the summer months.*

For many pond owners, the large lily pad leaves and beautiful lotuslike blooms of the water lily are the epitome of a water garden. There is such a wonderful variety of types, offering different colors, forms and even scent. However, it is important to choose varieties with care, as the large vigorous types are totally unsuitable for smaller pools. For the smallest ponds and tub and barrel gardens there are miniature lilies with a spread of about $12\text{in}^2(30\text{cm}^2)$ and these need a depth of water of only 4-9in(10-23cm). Slightly larger, and ideal for small to medium-sized pools, is the group classified as 'small lilies' , which have a spread of up to $3\text{ft}^2(0.3\text{m}^2)$. They require a planting depth of 6-15in (15-38cm). You can grow these smaller types on the marginal shelf or in plastic baskets, but make sure that the crown is well below ice level to prevent frost damage. The miniature varieties will need adequate protection in winter in cold climates.

Whatever the size of the pool, it is worth remembering that water lilies serve a very practical purpose as well as a decorative one; the spread of their leaves shades a large part of the water surface, offering shade and shelter for fish and depriving algae of sunlight. Without light and heat the algae cannot reproduce too rapidly and give you problems with green water. Do not forget that there is as much variety in the foliage of lilies as in the blooms, with many different shapes, colors and markings.

Left: The open cup, faintly scented 3.5in(9cm) flowers of Nymphaea *'Indiana' darken as they age to a dark apricot orange and finally red. The leaves are marbled with dark brown.*

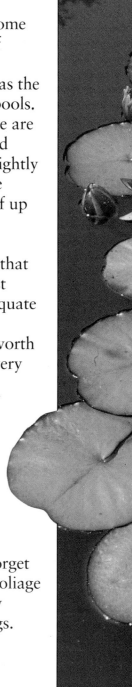

Below: *The hardy Nymphaea x laydekeri 'Fulgens' produces brilliant red, star-shaped blooms in summer, each 2-4in(5-10cm) across*

Right: *Nymphaea odorata minor. The sweetly scented flowers, up to 3.5in (9cm) across, are borne from mid to late summer above plain green foliage.*

Below: *Some water lilies, such as Nymphaea caroliniana 'Nivea' produce beautiful semi-double flowers. These are pure white and have a lovely scent. The pale green, deciduous leaves are also attractive.*

Other small lilies

pygmaea *'Alba' (white)*
'Laydekeri Liliacea'(pink)
'Laydekeri Purpurata'(red)
pygmaea *'Rubra'(red)*
candida*(white)*
'Ellisiana'(red), *'Froebeli'(red)*
'Aurora' (copper yellow turning to salmon orange, then red)
'Robinsoniana' (vermilion/orange)

Moderate water lilies

Choosing the right size lily for your pool is one thing; selecting the correct number of varieties you might reasonably grow in the space is another matter. It is easy to be tempted by too many different types, and lilies will not grow well if they are crowded. Alternatively, they will swamp the water surface. It can be difficult to calculate exactly how many plants you should allow yourself, as size and vigor vary considerably. Your water lily stockist should be able to estimate the final size of your chosen plant. As a general guideline, you can cover about 40 to 50 percent of the water surface, assuming that about 10 to 30 percent will be covered with other floating plants. The moderately sized water lilies suitable for small to medium pools usually require a planting depth of 6-18in(15-45cm) and will cover about 6-12ft²(0.6-1.1m²). After several years, these lilies may start to outgrow smaller pools. If you lift and divide them, this will reduce their growth and provide them with fresh nutrients.

Below: Nymphaea 'Rose Arey' is one of the most colorful lilies. Its scented cerise blooms with their starlike petals, display bright orange stamens tipped with yellow, and the purple leaves turn to green.

Above: Nymphaea 'Sultan' has deep red blooms that fade to pink as they reach the tips of the petals. The cluster of stamens is a warm golden color and the large flat leaves are a dark green.

Below: The pale orange and apricot blooms of Nymphaea 'Sioux', up to 5in(13cm) across, darken with age.

Water lily problems

Lilies can suffer from lily beetle or blackfly. Remove badly affected leaves and use a fish-safe insecticide or hose them into the water for the fish to eat. Crown rot may affect newly planted lilies; remove plant for treatment.

Right: *N. 'James Brydon' is prized for its crimson-pink peony-like blooms and purple leaves, which turn to dark green with a brown edge. The cup-shaped flowers have a delicate scent.*

Nymphaea 'Firecrest' is ideal for small to medium pools.

Below: *Nymphaea 'Firecrest' is aptly named; the center of each pretty pink bloom blazes with a cluster of golden stamens, streaked with orange and red, like tiny flames.*

Medium water lilies

It is worth considering medium-sized water lilies not just for average-sized pools, but also for larger water features where you might choose two medium lilies instead of only one of the larger, vigorous types. In that way, you could enjoy several different colors and types. This extensive group of lilies requires a planting depth of between 6 and 24in(15-60cm) and each plant can be expected to make a spread of foliage up to 12-15ft^2(1.1-1.3m^2).

As with the other hardy water lily groups, you will find a superb range of colors to chose from among the blooms, with star shapes and large double forms, too. As well as the classic snow-white, lilies are available in every shade of pink, from hot cerise to pale rose. There are really eye-catching, deep red lilies, golden yellows and even copper-orange varieties that change color as they age. Often, you will find that lilies are not an even color all over, but that the shade is densest towards the center of the bloom, fading almost to white at the tips of the petals. This color graduation only adds to their delicate charm.

Left: Nymphaea 'Pink Sensation' *is a relatively new introduction. Its pointed petals fade from a deep pink at the base to a silvery pink at the tips. The dark green leaves have an attractive bronze tinge.*

The pointed petals are a deep rosy red at the center, fading to pale pink flecked with a deeper pink towards the tips.

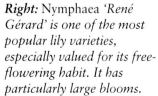

Right: Nymphaea 'René Gérard' *is one of the most popular lily varieties, especially valued for its free-flowering habit. It has particularly large blooms.*

Above: The cup-shaped, pale pink blooms of Nymphaea 'Formosa' are stippled with darker pink, and reach 3.75in(9.5cm) across. Faintly scented.

Above: For intensity of color, you cannot beat Nymphaea 'Escarboucle', whose large, long-lasting blooms are a stunning shade of crimson. The plant produces a mass of blooms throughout the flowering season.

Right: Known for its reliability, Nymphaea 'Marliacea Albida' grows vigorously and is free-flowering, producing plenty of large, white fragrant blooms among the contrasting dark green foliage.

Medium water lilies

Here we look at a further selection of medium water lilies, the most popular type for the majority of garden pools. Water lilies prefer a warm, sunny position, as their blooms tend to be smaller and paler when they grow in shade. Depending on the climate and levels of sunshine, most plants should start flowering as temperatures rise above 65°F(18°C) in early summer, the blooms opening in the morning and closing later in the afternoon. You may find that if the weather is particularly warm, the flowers will open earlier in the morning and close in the early afternoon. The blooms are often smaller and paler when the plant is young; in an older plant, poor flowers are more likely to be an indication that the plant is potbound or needs a dose of fertilizer. With such a greedy root system, lilies need large containers with plenty of rich aquatic potting mixture.

Right: For a really showy display, Nymphaea 'Mrs. Richmond' has huge blooms that are pale rose-pink on opening, deepening to a darker pink with age. The leaves are light green.

Left: Nymphaea 'Marliacea Rosea' is a deeper pink variety of the vigorous N. 'Marliacea Carnea'. It flowers white for the first year or so and then a rose-pink stain spreads up into the petals from the base of each bloom.

Right: N. 'Moorei' is similar to the popular N. 'Marliacea Chromatella', but is not quite as large or free-flowering. It has pretty primrose-yellow flowers spotted with brown. The foliage is spotted with purple on the undersides of each large leaf.

Below: The blooms of Nymphaea 'Attraction' are a deep wine color at the base of the central petals, graduating to almost white at the tips of the outer petals once established.

Below: Nymphaea odorata 'Alba' is a free-flowering medium-sized variety with pure white, cup-shaped blooms and a delicious scent. The bright apple green foliage is equally attractive.

Left: Vigorous Nymphaea 'Colonel A.J. Welch' is excellent for deep water. It has large, star-shaped, canary yellow blooms with narrow pointed petals. The flowers are not plentiful, but they stay open later in the afternoons.

Large water lilies

Large, vigorous water lily species really do need plenty of space, as they can spread to cover an area of anything between 15 and 25ft^2(1.3-2.3m^2) and require a water depth of 9-48in(23-120cm). They would quickly clog up smaller pools. Once established, any size of water lily will reward you with a succession of flowers through the summer, each bloom lasting three to five days before sinking below the surface. As well as having a strict preference concerning levels of sunshine and needing plenty of rich soil in order to flourish, water lilies dislike any disturbance of the water, so they are not suited to pools with a fountain or waterfall. If there is a slight flow of water through a natural lake or pond, you should be careful where you position your lilies and preferably plant them in containers that are easy to lift out of the water. You can then check the water lily stems to make sure that they are not slowing down the flow of water or encouraging silting up.

Left: Once the plant is established, N. 'Conqueror' bears large, wine-red blooms flecked with white. The petals become paler towards the tips. This is one lily that stays open in the evenings.

Right: N. 'Charles de Meurville' blooms early and has a long flowering season. It produces outsize wine-red flowers, each one up to 10in (25cm) across. The outer petals may be paler, opening to reveal a mass of golden stamens.

Below: N. 'Alba' is the classic white lily native to Europe and Asia. Its growth habit is so vigorous that it is really only suited to larger lakes and pools, where it makes a spread of mid-green flat leaves and cup-shaped blooms with bright yellow centers.

Right: Large white globular blooms with prominent green sepals identify N. tuberosa 'Richardsonii', It is an improved form of a native North American lily and is suited only to larger pools. The large round leaves are an attractive apple-green color.

Planting a water lily

Water lilies are greedy feeders, especially the more vigorous types, so they appreciate the largest container you have room for and a soil depth of at least 6in(15cm). Containers come in various types and sizes, including the familiar perforated baskets specially designed for aquatic plants, but also as wide, solid-sided bowls. Spring is the best time to transplant lilies, as they will have just started their growing season and this gives the plants plenty of time to establish themselves before becoming dormant. A reasonably mature specimen could be expected to flower in its first season, although the first blooms may be smaller and paler than expected. It is important not to cover the growing point of the lily tuber or rhizome. The crown should stand proud of the soil or gravel. Lower the heavy baskets carefully to the correct level, using bricks, blocks or upturned baskets as supports. Start young plants near the water surface - allow, say, 6-10in(15-25cm) over the crown and lower them gradually as sufficient leaves develop. As a guide, you should not be able to see open leaves below the water. It may be several years before you can fully lower deep water lilies to 3ft(90cm) or more.

1 The latest lily baskets have louvered sides with special perforations that do not require lining. Start to fill the container with a suitable aquatic potting mixture.

2 Carefully lay the lily onto the potting mixture and begin to top up the basket with more mixture, firming in the plant as you proceed.

3 When the basket is full, cover the surface of the potting mixture with gravel or small stones to keep the soil in place once the basket is lowered into the water.

The layer of small stones will also help to prevent fish from disturbing the plant.

4 *The finished container is ready to be lowered into the pool. Return the plant to water as soon as possible after planting to ensure its survival.*

Make sure that the crown of the plant is above the level of soil in the basket.

5 *Place sufficient bricks in the pool to bring the basket to the required level below the surface of the water. See plant label for planting depth.*

6 *Lower the container carefully into the water so that it rests securely on the bricks. Do not drop it in; you may damage the plant and pond liner.*

Feeding water lilies

Once the lilies are established, they will begin to deplete the natural resources in the planting mixture and will benefit from a regular feed.

Water lily food comes in powdered, tablet or sachet form; simply press this into the top of the basket. Follow the maker's instructions.

Fertilizer in small bags

Powdered fertilizer

7 *If it has been correctly planted, the lily leaves will eventually float up to rest on the water surface. Place young plants in shallow water at first.*

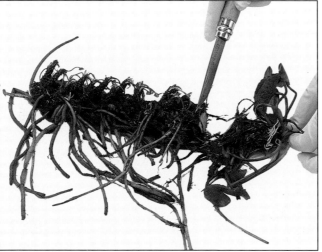

1 Using a sharp knife or scalpel blade, sever the main plant cleanly from its fleshy rhizome. It is a good idea to wear gloves when handling lily roots, as some species can stain your hands.

2 Now, with your knife, begin removing all the spurting 'eyes' along the rhizomatic tuber. Put the eyes carefully to one side until you are ready to pot them up.

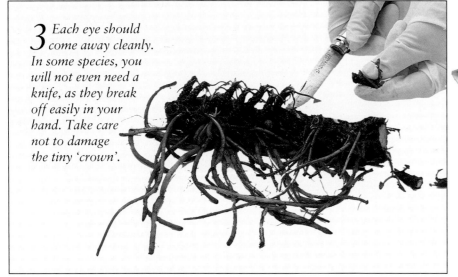

3 Each eye should come away cleanly. In some species, you will not even need a knife, as they break off easily in your hand. Take care not to damage the tiny 'crown'.

Propagating a water lily

Water lilies can be expensive to buy, so if you have a mature specimen that is starting to heave itself out of the container, it is worth the trouble to propagate new plants from the old rootstock. A lily will be fairly old and well established before it is suitable for propagation. Lift it carefully free of the water and lever or cut away the container. There are two types of growth; those that produce a tuberlike rhizome that grows horizontally, and others that grow from a knobby upright rootstock. It is important to remember which type you have, because you must plant the rootstock at the same angle. As well as being able to propagate plants from new sections of growth or side shoots on the old rootstock, you could propagate each small 'eye' - tiny budding plants that appear along the length of the tuber - to produce more than a dozen plants from a single old one. These small plantlets should become established within about two years.

Below: Nymphaea 'Marliacea' is a good reliable lily bearing pretty pink blooms and a delicate scent throughout the summer. Different varieties offer varying shades of pink.

Having taken out the 'eyes', you can now pot up this part of the plant, as shown on pages 98-99.

4 *A single rhizome from a mature lily plant might yield as many as twelve to twenty new plants. This will be far more than you need, so swap with family and friends.*

Each of these 'eyes' will grow into a complete new plant.

5 *Press each new plantlet into a tray of moist aquatic potting mixture, leaving the 'crown' of the small plant exposed. Allow space for a layer of small stones to be added to stop the soil floating out of the tray.*

6 *A single tray can hold as many as twelve new plants. Each plant will take a couple of years to grow to a size suitable for planting out. The plants will need transferring to larger containers as they develop.*

7 *Cover the potting mix with small stones, taking care not to bury the small plants completely. Submerge the tray in a tank or a large bowl of water until the plantlets mature.*

You can slice or break off the 'eyes' on the discarded rootstock to propagate more plants, as shown on pages 96-7.

1 *Using a sharp blade and keeping the plant moist, slice cleanly through the rootstock to sever the new growth and create a fresh plant.*

2 *Remove the long anchor roots from the new plant, making a clean cut close to the crown. Leave the smaller roots intact.*

Trimming a water lily rootstock

Once you have the rootstock in your hands, you might find it useful to rinse the plant gently in cold water to remove the excess mud so that you can see more clearly what you are doing. It is important not to let the plant dry out while you are working on it, so have a watering can nearby to keep it wet. Cut the rootstock with a sharp knife or scalpel blade to avoid bruising. Your first cut will be to remove the newest section of growth, which will develop and become established more quickly than one of the 'eyes'. When you make the cut, allow about 3-8in(7.5-20cm) of rootstock. Trim away most of the long anchoring roots from this piece, leaving just a few smaller roots to provide the plant with nutrients. Also trim off any dead tissue and most of the old leaves, since these will not grow and might make the plant too buoyant and even lift it out of the container. The new plant will produce fresh leaves and roots all the quicker for this rather drastic treatment.

These small white roots will develop and sustain the new plant.

Severed anchor roots

The original plant crown will form the basis of the new one.

3 *Removing the old roots encourages the plant to grow new, stronger ones, and will prevent the old roots rotting and infecting the crown.*

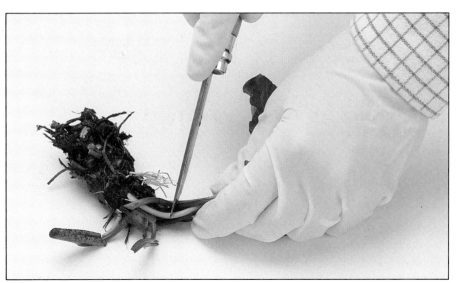

5 Gently plant the newly prepared lily crown in a perforated container of aquatic potting mix, using the same technique as for any new lily plant.

4 Trim the leaves from the top of the plant in the same way. If left on, they will die back, putting the plant at risk from infection.

6 A layer of small stones sprinkled on the surface of the potting mix will help to keep the soil and the plants in place once they are submerged in the pond or pool.

7 The new plant is now potted up in its container and ready to be submerged in the pool or nursery tank until the lily has become established.

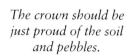

The crown should be just proud of the soil and pebbles.

99

Creating a water feature in a barrel

If you would really like a pond feature, but have no room in the garden or on the patio, or if excavations and major building work are impractical, you can always set up a miniature pool in a pot, tub or other suitable container. Providing they are scaled down, you can have all the features you set your heart on; water lilies, marginal plants, fish and even a tiny, sparkling fountain. The finished tub can be a real focal point and provide hours of pleasure for very little outlay in terms of time and money, as well as space. Any waterproof container is suitable, from a large cut-down barrel to a small terracotta or plastic patio pot. The only real proviso is that the chosen container has not been treated with any poisonous or fungicidal chemicals that might damage plants and fish. Some garden centers sell tub kits that come complete with everything you need, even a selection of plants, to be assembled at home. Alternatively, buy a ready-made bubble fountain in a stone or terracotta container, with plants and pebbles installed for an instant moving water feature.

2 Since the wooden barrel is not waterproof, the first task is to line it. Use a large piece of proper pond liner and push it firmly down inside.

3 Trim off some of the excess at this stage, but leave plenty around the edges to allow for it to settle down further as you add water and bricks.

1 These are the ingredients to make a stunning water feature in a tub. It is a good idea to set out what you plan to include in the final display before you start work. This also gives you the chance to see whether the elements will look good together.

Make sure this tube is firmly pushed into the pump.

4 Put the pump in now. This is a small, mains-powered model ideally suited to the size of the display. Place it on a brick for stability and to bring it up to the correct height.

5 Place a layer of bricks around the inside of the barrel. These will provide platforms to support the plant pots and stones. Use hard bricks sold for paving; they are more durable in water.

6 Add some cobbles to fill in the spaces between the bricks. These will help to stabilize the piles of bricks and will also stop the pump moving around once the feature is operating.

7 Add a top layer of paving bricks. These will support the large stones and plant pots of the final display. Build the bricks up in stable patterns to avoid problems later on.

8 Now add the large stones that will form the visible part of the feature. Rounded boulders such as these not only look attractive but will also stand continuous immersion in water.

9 Add water until it reaches the base of the boulders. This will leave enough expansion room to add the plants and final stones.

Planting up the barrel

1 If you want to neaten things up a bit at this stage you can trim off more of the liner. The weight of the water will have pushed the liner into its final position.

Here we show how to plant up the barrel prepared on pages 100-101. Of course, all kinds of troughs, pots, tubs and barrels are suitable for planting up in this way. Just make sure that they are painted inside with a sealant or lined with butyl rubber or plastic pond liner to ensure that they are watertight. Do remember that once filled with water, a few plants and any other water features you may chose, such as an ornament or fountain, the tub or pot is going to be extremely heavy, so decide on its final position while it is empty and plant it up in situ. If you are going to have to move the feature, place the container on a low platform with lockable casters for mobility. A water feature in a tub makes an excellent focal point for a dull corner of the garden or patio, where it might be raised on such a platform or a few bricks for extra prominence. Alternatively, stand it on a bed of pebbles or gravel or surround it with large stones and pots of lush plants to reinforce the watery effect. To show the tub at its best, make sure you position it against a suitable backdrop, such as a wall, fence or plain greenery. Large pebbles or a wall behind are also useful for installing concealed spouts for moving water effects to enhance the feature.

2 Now begin to add the plants. Since they will be immersed in water, you can choose from a wide range of marginal plants that thrive in these conditions. Pot them into the plastic mesh baskets that you use for the pond.

Smooth stones or boulders look best in small pools.

3 If the display has a definite front view, then plan the planting with this in mind. Adding this low growing water forget-me-not towards the front will work well with the tall water buttercup at the back of the barrel.

4 Once the planting is complete, you can add more stones to fill in spaces that seem to 'appear'. Adding another boulder here creates a better display. Be careful not to dislodge the outlet pipe of the pump as you move heavy items around.

5 Add cobbles and pebbles to match the color range and shape of the boulders. This helps the feature to look more like the bank of a natural stream. By now the barrel is very heavy and you should be working on it in its final location in the garden setting.

Lysimachia thyrsiflora

Ranunculus flammula

Iris versicolor 'Blue Light'

Myosotis palustris

Epimedium x youngianum 'Roseum' (Not a marginal but would look attractive close to the barrel.)

Primula veris (Not suitable for inside the barrel, but this bog garden plant thrives in damp soil.)

6 This is the final display with a three-tier spray fountain head fitted to the pump. The edges of the liner have been trimmed neatly around the top of the barrel.

7 If you prefer a bell-shaped effect then fit the appropriate head. Be careful not to pull out the central tube of the pump when changing heads.

Small water features

A delightful miniature pond or water garden is easily assembled using a selection of scaled-down plants and features. The secret is not to choose too many of these or the effect will be overcrowded and lose some of its impact. Providing the pool or tub is deep enough for a small fountain pump, you can devise all kinds of interesting moving water effects, from a simple jet to tiny babbling and dome sprays. If you have small children, the reservoir can be concealed below a bed of pebbles or an old millstone. Alternatively, a wall-mounted spout or simple dish can make a simple but eye-catching, self-contained feature in the smallest of spaces. Choose ornaments that are in proportion to your feature and position these close by the pool if not actually in the water. If you are more interested in plants, then there are many dwarf varieties to choose from, including miniature water lilies. Plants will probably need regular trimming to keep them in check.

Left: *A simple planting scheme combined with an unusually detailed mosaic fountain base give this small circular pool maximum impact.*

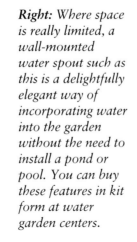

Right: Where space is really limited, a wall-mounted water spout such as this is a delightfully elegant way of incorporating water into the garden without the need to install a pond or pool. You can buy these features in kit form at water garden centers.

Above: Japanese garden designers are the masters of small moving water features like this shishi-odoshi, originally designed to scare deer from the garden. With its gentle trickling and regular 'tock' as the pivoted bamboo hits the rock, this relaxing feature could form part of an oriental area with bamboos and Japanese-style ornaments.

Left: The sense of movement and the variety of shape and color in the wet stones are the simple ingredients that give this tiny bubble fountain feature its huge appeal.

Right: An old barrel, partially sunk into the ground, makes an excellent miniature pond that might be sited anywhere in the garden or on the patio.

Index to Plants

Page numbers in **bold** indicate major text references. Page numbers in *italics* indicate captions and annotations to photographs. Other text entries are shown in normal type.

Credits

The majority of the photographs featured in this book have been taken by Neil Sutherland and are © Colour Library Books. The publishers wish to thank the following photographers for providing additional photographs, credited here by page number and position on the page, i.e. (B)Bottom, (T)Top, (C)Center, (BL)Bottom left, etc.

Gillian Beckett: 38(BR), 39(C), 49(TC), 54(B), 67(TL), 70(BL, TC, TR), 72(TR), 74(BL), 78(BL), 96(BR)
Pat Brindley: 47(TL), 49(TR), 53(TR), 54(TR), 55(TL)
Eric Crichton 12(T,B), 17(TC), 19(CR), 20(TR), 24(T), 25(B), 26(TR), 46(BL), 63(BL), 64(L,BR), 65(TL),
66(T), 67(BR), 68(BL), 69(TR), 70(BR, T), 74(TR, BR), 77(TL), 79(TR, BR), 81(BL), 84-5(C), 87(B), 90(TR),
92-3(CB)
Ron & Christine Foord: 45(TC), 72(B)
John Glover: Half-title page, Credits, 13(TL, TR, BL, BR), 14(T), 16(TR, BL, BR), 17(L), 26(BR), 27(R),
32(BR), 75(TL), 88(L), 104(BL, BR), 105(TL, B)
Ideas into Print: 16(CR)
S & O Mathews: 26-7(C), 35(BR), 76(T), 91(BR), 92(BL), 93(T, BR)
Clive Nichols: 10, 18(T), 89(TL), 105(TR)
Maurice Nimmo: 47(TR), 50(TR)
Natural Image/Robin Fletcher: 68(T), 73(TL) Natural Image/Bob Gibbons: 42(T), 44, 51(T), 52(BL) 75(TR)
Natural Image/Liz Gibbons: 53(TL) Natural Image/Jean Hall: 69(TL)
Daan Smit: 77(TR)
Stapeley Water Gardens: 84(TL), 85(BR), 86(BL, BR), 87(TR), 88(BR), 89(B) 90(BL), 91(TR), 93(BR)
Elizabeth Whiting & Associates: 22-3(TC)

Acknowledgments

The publishers would like to thank Stapeley Water Gardens, near Nantwich in Cheshire, for providing plants and photographic facilities during the production of this book. Thanks are particularly due to Maria Farmer, Chris Adams, Kim Clarkson, Kevin Walley, Ron Hampson, Barry Sharps and Sarah Davies. The publishers would also like to thank Simon Chapman (Prototype Communications) and Hozelock for supplying pumps and other aquatic equipment for photography. The following companies provided liner and underlay samples for photography: Midland Butyl Liners, Bradshaws, Glass Art Pools, Hozelock.